AAT

Accounting Systems and Controls

Level 4
Professional Diploma in
Accounting
Course Book
For assessments to
June 2023

Fifth edition 2021

ISBN 9781 5097 3935 6
ISBN (for internal use only) 9781 5097 3934 9

British Library Cataloguing-in-Publication Data
A catalogue record for this book is available from the British Library

Published by

BPP Learning Media Ltd
BPP House, Aldine Place
142-144 Uxbridge Road
London W12 8AA

www.bpp.com/learningmedia

Printed in the United Kingdom

Your learning materials, published by BPP Learning Media Ltd, are printed on paper obtained from traceable sustainable sources.

Contents

		Page
Introduction to the course		iv
Skills bank		x
Chapter 1	Introduction to the organisation	1
Chapter 2	The accounting function	25
Chapter 3	Accounting systems	45
Chapter 4	Internal control systems	63
Chapter 5	Monitoring controls and detecting fraud	89
Chapter 6	Making changes to systems	115
Activity answers		139
Test your learning: answers		189
Cookridge & Cookridge Carpets Ltd (CCC) scenario and analysis		197
Glossary of terms		203
Bibliography		205
Index		207

Introduction to the course

Syllabus overview

The purpose of the unit is to enable students to demonstrate their understanding of the role of the accounting function in an organisation and the importance of internal controls in minimising the risk of loss. Students will undertake an evaluation of an accounting system to identify weaknesses and assess the impact of those weaknesses on the operation of the organisation.

They will then make recommendations to address the weaknesses having regard for cost/benefit, sustainability and the impact of those recommendations on users of the accounting system. *Accounting Systems and Controls* is only examined as part of the synoptic assessment. Therefore, this unit enables students to consolidate and apply the knowledge and understanding gained from the mandatory Level 4 units of *Financial Statements of Limited Companies, Management Accounting: Budgeting* and *Management Accounting: Decision and Control* as well as the knowledge obtained during this *Accounting Systems and Controls* course.

When organisations have a planned change in policy there will be a transition period, which will present its own challenges. Students need to be able to review a planned change in policy, identify potential problem areas while one system is being changed to another and make suitable recommendations to ensure that the integrity of the accounting system is maintained.

The accounting system affects all areas of an organisation and should be capable of producing information to assist management with decision making, monitoring and control, as well as producing financial information to meet statutory obligations. In this unit, students will demonstrate analytical and problem-solving skills, exercising judgement to make informed recommendations. These are practical skills that are essential to the accounting technician.

Accounting Systems and Controls requires students to have a sound understanding of management accounting and financial accounting information requirements, and the way that the accounting function needs to support both areas.

Test specification for Level 4 Synoptic assessment

Assessment method	Marking type	Duration of assessment
Computer based synoptic assessment	Partially computer / partially human marked	3 hours

Assessment objectives and Learning outcomes	Weighting
1 Demonstrate an understanding of the roles and responsibilities of the accounting function within an organisation and examine ways of preventing and detecting fraud and systemic weaknesses **Accounting Systems and Controls** LO1 Demonstrate an understanding of the role and responsibilities of the accounting function within an organisation LO2 Evaluate internal control systems	20%
2 Evaluate budgetary reporting and its effectiveness in controlling and improving organisational performance **Accounting Systems and Controls** LO1 Demonstrate an understanding of the role and responsibilities of the accounting function within an organisation LO2 Evaluate internal control systems LO3 Evaluate an organisation's accounting system and underpinning procedures **Management Accounting: Budgeting** LO3 Demonstrate how budgeting can improve organisational performance **Management Accounting: Decision and Control** LO1 Analyse a range of costing techniques to support the management accounting function of an organisation LO2 Calculate and use standard costing to improve performance	15%
3 Evaluate an organisation's accounting control systems and procedures **Accounting Systems and Controls** LO2 Evaluate internal control systems LO3 Evaluate an organisation's accounting system and underpinning procedures	15%

Assessment objectives and Learning outcomes	Weighting
4 Analyse an organisation's decision making and control using management accounting tools **Accounting Systems and Controls** LO1 Demonstrate an understanding of the role and responsibilities of the accounting function within an organisation LO2 Evaluate internal control systems LO3 Evaluate an organisation's accounting system and underpinning procedures LO4 Analyse recommendations made to improve an organisation's accounting system **Management Accounting: Decision and Control** LO2 Calculate and use standard costing to improve performance LO4 Use appropriate financial and non-financial performance techniques to aid decision making LO5 Evaluate a range of cost management techniques to enhance value and aid decision making	15%
5 Analyse an organisation's decision making and control using ratio analysis **Accounting Systems and Controls** LO1 Demonstrate an understanding of the role and responsibilities of the accounting function within an organisation LO2 Evaluate internal control systems LO4 Analyse recommendations made to improve an organisation's accounting system **Financial Statements of Limited Companies** LO1 Demonstrate an understanding of the reporting frameworks and ethical principles that underpin financial reporting LO5 Interpret financial statements using ratio analysis **Management Accounting: Decision and Control** LO4 Use appropriate financial and non-financial performance techniques to aid decision making	20%

Assessment objectives and Learning outcomes	Weighting
6 Analyse the internal controls of an organisation and make recommendations	15%
Accounting Systems and Controls	
LO1 Demonstrate an understanding of the role and responsibilities of the accounting function within an organisation	
LO2 Evaluate internal control systems	
LO3 Evaluate an organisation's accounting system and underpinning procedures	
LO4 Analyse recommendations made to improve an organisation's accounting system	
Financial Statements of Limited Companies	
LO1 Demonstrate an understanding of the reporting frameworks and ethical principles that underpin financial reporting	
Management Accounting: Budgeting	
LO3 Demonstrate how budgeting can improve organisational performance	
Management Accounting: Decision and Control	
LO4 Use appropriate financial and non-financial performance techniques to aid decision making	
LO5 Evaluate a range of cost management techniques to enhance value and aid decision making	
Total	**100%**

Assessment structure

3 hours duration

Competency is 70%

*Note that this is only a guideline as to what might come up. The format and content of each task may vary from what we have listed below.

Your assessment will consist of 6 tasks

Task	Expected content	Max marks	Unit ref	Study complete
Task 1	Role of accounting function; preventing and detecting fraud and systemic weaknesses	20	Accounting Systems and Controls	
Task 2	Effectiveness of budgetary reporting in controlling and improving performance	15	Accounting Systems and Controls Management Accounting: Budgeting Management Accounting: Decision and Control	
Task 3	Accounting control systems and procedures	15	Accounting Systems and Controls	
Task 4	Management accounting tools for decision making and control	15	Accounting Systems and Controls Management Accounting: Decision and Control	

Task	Expected content	Max marks	Unit ref	Study complete
Task 5	Ratio analysis for decision making and control	20	Accounting Systems and Controls Financial Statements of Limited Companies Management Accounting: Decision and Control	
Task 6	Analysis of and recommendations for internal controls	15	Accounting Systems and Controls Financial Statements of Limited Companies Management Accounting: Budgeting Management Accounting: Decision and Control	

Skills bank

Our experience of preparing students for this type of assessment suggests that to obtain competency, you will need to develop a number of key skills.

What do I need to know to do well in the AAT *Professional Diploma in Accounting Synoptic Assessment?*

Accounting Systems and Controls is part of the Level 4 AAT *Professional Diploma in Accounting Synoptic Assessment.* This assessment also includes significant elements of the other mandatory units at Level 4 – *Management Accounting: Budgeting, Management Accounting: Decision and Control,* and *Financial Statements of Limited Companies* – for which you should refer to the relevant Course Books, as well as the practice assessments in the Level 4 AAT *Professional Diploma in Accounting Synoptic Assessment* Question Bank.

To be successful in the assessment you need to:

- Understand the role and responsibilities of the accounting function within an organisation

- Evaluate internal control systems

- Evaluate an organisation's accounting system and underpinning procedures

- Analyse recommendations made to improve an organisation's accounting system

Assumed knowledge

Accounting Systems and Controls is a **mandatory** unit and builds on the fundamental concepts and techniques introduced and developed throughout Levels 2 and 3.

It is **essential** that you have thorough knowledge of, and have completed studying for the following units **prior** to commencing your AAT *Professional Diploma in Accounting Synoptic Assessment* (PDSY):

- *Financial Statements of Limited Companies (FSLC)*
- *Management Accounting: Decision and Control (MDCL)*
- *Management Accounting: Budgeting (MABU)*

In addition, the AAT have restrictions in place which do not allow you to sit the AAT *Professional Diploma in Accounting Synoptic Assessment* (PDSY) until the assessments for the other three mandatory units at Level 4 have been scheduled.

The final element in the AAT *Professional Diploma in Accounting Synoptic Assessment* is introducing the *Accounting Systems and Controls* unit.

Questions will be asked, in line with the Assessment Objectives and Learning Outcomes, which cover elements of all four of the above units. It is therefore, imperative that you are confident in your knowledge and application of the skills learned in those units, and of those at Level 3.

Assessment style

In the synoptic assessment you will complete tasks by:

1   Entering narrative by selecting from drop-down menus of narrative options known as **picklists**

2   Using **drag and drop** menus to enter narrative

3   Typing in numbers, known as **gapfill** entry

4   Entering **ticks**

5   Entering **dates** by selecting from a calendar

6   Entering extended **written answers** for human marking.

You must familiarise yourself with the style of the online questions and the AAT software before taking the synoptic assessment. As part of your revision, log in to the **AAT website** and attempt their **online practice assessments**.

Each question style is explained in more detail below.

Picklists

Here you need to answer questions by selecting the appropriate wording from a list of options. These options will be given in a drop down box and be presented in alphabetical order.

Gapfill entry

Many tasks will require you to calculate a specific number and then enter it into the proforma / solution box on-screen. This is known as gapfill entry.

An example is given below taken from the AAT *Professional Diploma in Accounting Synoptic Assessment* Sample Assessment Task 5:

(a) Complete the scorecard by calculating:
- **the FOUR missing ratios**
- **the working capital cycle.**

SL Products Ltd Scorecard	Year ended 31 Dec 20X1	Year ended 31 Dec 20X2
Profitability & gearing (correct to 1 dp):		
Gross profit %	28.4%	%
Operating profit %	6.3%	2.2%
Return on capital employed	17.5%	%
Gearing	16.6%	20.1%
Liquidity ratios (correct to 1 dp):		
Current ratio	1.8 : 1	: 1
Acid test / Quick ratio	0.8 : 1	: 1
Working capital days (correct to nearest day):		
Inventory holding period	92 days	94 days
Trade receivables collection period	54 days	53 days
Trade payables payment period	86 days	90 days
Working capital cycle	60 days	days

(10 marks)

To calculate the number to include in the scorecard you must consider both:

- The numbers in the scorecard, given in the scenario; and
- Further information (eg the extracts from the financial statements provided)

Note that in the assessment, any further information will be provided to you through 'pop-up' boxes. It is **very** important to log in to the AAT website are familiarise yourself with the style of the exam, well before you sit the real assessment!

Entering ticks

Several short-form objective style questions will require you to indicate your answer by entering a tick. For example:

- 'Yes' or 'no'
- 'True' or 'false'
- ticking to indicate your choice of number.

The following question appears in the AAT *Professional Diploma in Accounting Synoptic Assessment* sample assessment, Task 1 part (d):

(d) Why should the Accounts Receivable (Sales Ledger) control account be reconciled to the individual account be reconciled to the individual Accounts Receivable (Sales Ledger) balances?

	✓
To detect posting errors in the Accounts Receivable Ledger.	
To detect missing sales invoices.	
To detect posting errors in the Cash Book.	
To detect missing credit notes.	

(2 marks)

You may need to read the scenario and requirement several times in order to understand the requirement before you enter a tick in the correct box.

Extended writing skills

The Level 4 *Professional Diploma in Accounting Synoptic Assessment* will be assessing **application** as well as knowledge of the four mandatory units studied at this level. There will be a number of questions which require an extended written response. It is recommended that you follow these tips to support their learning for this assessment:

- Practice the questions in the *Professional Diploma in Accounting Synoptic Assessment* Question Bank and from within this Course Book.

- Analyse your answers against the sample answers given. Consider whether your answer is answering the given question, whether your response is specific to the given scenario and whether you can support your judgements using figures and information provided from the scenario.

- The AAT has useful question and style tips on their website, which can be found at: www.aat.org.uk/training/study-support/search. In particular, the 'Writing skills' and 'Synoptic assessment support' offer useful advice towards preparing your writing techniques for this assessment.

- Complete the practice assessments which will enable you to test your time management skills as well as practice your extended writing abilities.

The extended written answers may be short answers, requiring one or two sentences, such as this extract from Task 3 in the AAT *Professional Diploma in Accounting Synoptic Assessment* sample assessment:

(a) Identify FIVE systemic weaknesses in the company's internal controls for the procedures underpinning its accounting for sales, including its Accounts Receivable Ledger and banking procedures.

(5 marks)

(b) Explain how EACH weakness may cause the company problems. (10 marks)

Weakness	Potential problem for the company

In this case, the candidates are being asked for five weaknesses and how they may cause problems for the company. Here, there is one mark available for the identification of the weakness and a further two marks to explain why this may be an issue for the company. Therefore, sufficient information must be written to explain the issue and why this may be the case, but there is no need to write an overly long explanation as the maximum points available are three marks per valid weakness.

Alternatively, the answer may require more detail, and a larger amount of space will be available to input your answer. Look carefully at the marking allocation to give an indication of the level of detail required.

Read the question carefully

The main verbs used for these type of question requirements are:

Identify – analyse and select for presentation

Explain – set out in detail the meaning of

Discuss – by argument, discuss the pros and cons

READ the question carefully

It is important to read the question carefully to identify exactly what is being asked of you. It is a good idea to highlight key words and all verbs as this will ensure you answer the question that is being asked, not the question you think they should ask!

PLAN your answer

Once you have established the requirement, note down what you know about the topic, **relevant** to what is being asked (key words only). It is a good idea to do this on a piece of paper so you can eliminate irrelevant knowledge and formulate a logical answer when you enter it on screen.

Analysis and interpretation

With the **analysis and interpretation questions**, you should:

1   Read the question carefully, identifying the answer format required (eg memo, report etc).

2   Make sure you have scrap paper available so that you can plan your answer.

3   Identify the ratios you are asked to analyse. Note them down on scrap paper to ensure you don't miss any out!

4   For each ratio, you should be commenting on whether it is better / worse than the industry average / prior year / other company; why it is better / worse; what it tells you about the company; and how to improve it (if applicable).

5   If you are asked to give a conclusion or recommendation, you must do this! Marks will be available for this part of the answer

Before answering the question set, you need to carefully review the scenario given in order to consider what questions need to be answered, and what needs to be discussed. A simple framework that could be used to answer the question is as follows:

- Point – make the point
- Evidence – use information from the scenario as evidence
- Explain – explain why the evidence links to the point

For example if an assessment task asked us to explain the Net Profit Margin we could answer as follows:

1   Point – the NPM tell us the amount of net profit earned per pound of revenue

2   Evidence – in this case the company is performing better than the competitor as we have a higher net profit percentage than Company Y

3   Explain – which means that/the consequences are …

Recommendations are normally also required, to provide guidance on how to proceed:

1   Recommendation – therefore we should invest in the company

This approach provides a formula or framework that can be followed, to answer written questions:

The NPM tells us that (Point) …. in this case the company is (Evidence) ….. which means that (Explain) …. so we should/should not …. (Recommendation).

You must familiarise yourself with the style of the online questions and the AAT software before taking the assessment. As part of your revision, login to the **AAT website** and attempt their **online practice assessments**.

Introduction to the assessment

The question practice you do will prepare you for the format of tasks you will see in the AAT *Professional Diploma in Accounting Synoptic Assessment*

Information on the scenario for your AAT *Professional Diploma in Accounting Synoptic Assessment* is issued in advance of the assessment as pre-seen material. You must make sure you are familiar with the relevant pre-seen material before sitting your assessment. The pre-seen scenario for the live assessment should be downloaded from the AAT website (www.aat.org.uk/training/study-support/search).

Note that the scenario is also included as a pop-up in the live assessment, but it is strongly advised that you familiarise yourself with the information prior to the assessment.

It is also useful to familiarise yourself with the other introductory information you **may** be given at the start of the assessment. The following is provided at the beginning of the sample synoptic assessment:

Assessment information

Read the scenario carefully before attempting the questions, you can return to it at any time by clicking on the 'Introduction' button at the bottom of the screen.

Complete all 6 tasks.

Answer the questions in the spaces provided. For tasks requiring extended written answers, the answer box will expand to fit your answer.

You must use a full stop to indicate a decimal point. For example, write 100.57 NOT 100,57 OR 100 57.

Both minus signs and brackets can be used to indicate negative numbers UNLESS task instructions say otherwise.

You may use a comma to indicate a number in the thousands, but you don't have to. For example, 10000 and 10,000 are both okay.

Where the date is relevant, it is given in the task data.

Information

The total time for this paper is 3 hours.

This assessment has a total of 6 tasks which are divided into sub-tasks.

There are 100 marks available in this assessment.

The marks available for each task are shown at the top of each task.

The marks for each sub-task are shown alongside the relevant sub-task.

The data you need to complete each task is contained within that task or through the pop-up windows provided on the task page; you will not need to refer to your answers for previous tasks.

Advice

Read each question carefully before you start to answer it.

Attempt all questions.

You can return to a task at any time during the assessment to check your answers.

1   Attempt as many tasks as possible in the **Question Bank**. There are plenty of assessment-style tasks which are excellent preparation for the real synoptic assessment.

2   Always **check** through your own answers as you will in the real assessment, before looking at the solutions in the back of the Question Bank.

Key to icons

 Key term — A key definition which is important to be aware of for the assessment

 Formula to learn — A formula you will need to learn as it will not be provided in the assessment

 Formula provided — A formula which is provided within the assessment and generally available as a pop-up on screen

 Activity — An example which allows you to apply your knowledge to the technique covered in the Course Book. The solution is provided at the end of the chapter

 Illustration — A worked example which can be used to review and see how an assessment question could be answered

 Assessment focus point — A high priority point for the assessment

 Open book reference — Where use of an open book will be allowed for the assessment

Real life examples — A practical real life scenario

BPP LEARNING MEDIA

AAT qualifications

The material in this book may support the following AAT qualifications:

AAT Professional Diploma in Accounting Level 4 and AAT Professional Diploma in Accounting at SCQF Level 8.

Supplements

From time to time we may need to publish supplementary materials to one of our titles. This can be for a variety of reasons, from a small change in the AAT unit guidance to new legislation coming into effect between editions.

You should check our supplements page regularly for anything that may affect your learning materials. All supplements are available free of charge on our supplements page on our website at:

www.bpp.com/learning-media/about/students

Improving material and removing errors

There is a constant need to update and enhance our study materials in line with both regulatory changes and new insights into the assessments.

From our team of authors BPP appoints a subject expert to update and improve these materials for each new edition.

Their updated draft is subsequently technically checked by another author and from time to time non-technically checked by a proofreader.

We are very keen to remove as many numerical errors and narrative typos as we can but given the volume of detailed information being changed in a short space of time we know that a few errors will sometimes get through our net.

We apologise in advance for any inconvenience that an error might cause. We continue to look for new ways to improve these study materials and would welcome your suggestions. If you have any comments about this book, please use the review form at the back.

These learning materials are based on the qualification specification released by the AAT in January 2020.

Introduction to the organisation

1

Learning outcomes

1.1	**Discuss the purpose, structure and organisation of the accounting function** • The difference between financial and management accounting • The importance of ethics and sustainability within the accounting function
1.2	**Discuss the purpose of the key financial reports and their use by a range of stakeholders** • The purpose and content of statutory financial statements • The key external stakeholders of an organisation • How financial information is used by both internal and external stakeholders • The importance of ethical information and sustainability practices to internal and external stakeholders • The following types of financial report: – Income statement – Statement of financial position – Statement of cash flow
1.3	**Examine the impact of relevant regulations affecting the accounting function** • Identify the types of regulations that affect the accounting function
3.1	**Examine an organisation's accounting system and its effectiveness** • Identify the varying financial information requirements of stakeholders (payroll, sales accounting, purchases accounting, general ledger, cash book and costing systems)

Assessment context

Assessment of these topics will be included within a number of tasks in the AAT *Professional Diploma in Accounting* synoptic assessment at Level 4.

Qualification context

Statutory financial statements are also covered in the *Financial Statements for Limited Companies* unit at Level 4. Different types of organisation and accounting regulations are covered at an introductory level in *Final Accounts Preparation* at Level 3. Management need to make ethical decisions when making strategic and operational decisions. These are covered in the Level 4 unit *Management Accounting: Decision and Control*.

Business context

Accountants need to understand the purpose of the internal and external reports they create, and how this information will be used by a variety of stakeholders. When preparing reports you must consider why the information is required, so that it can be provided in the appropriate format and with the appropriate level of detail, bearing in mind the needs of the reader(s) of the report.

Chapter overview

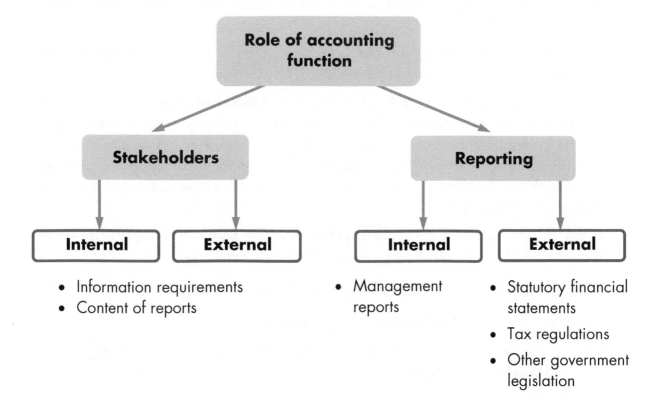

- Information requirements
- Content of reports

- Management reports

- Statutory financial statements
- Tax regulations
- Other government legislation
- Mission statement
- Corporate social reporting (CSR)
- Sustainability
- Ethical
- Other regulations

Introduction

In this chapter we look at some of the basic principles of the *Accounting Systems and Controls* unit.

The *Financial Statements of Limited Companies* module has already covered the different types of organisation in detail.

Organisations are heavily influenced by their **stakeholders** – individuals or groups who are in some way affected by the organisation's actions. Stakeholders can be categorised as either internal or external. Those running an organisation, and its accounting function, must consider the varying needs of its stakeholders when making decisions. A more detailed review of the accounting function is covered in Chapter 2.

In this chapter, we evaluate the **importance** of the financial statements and how they are used by both internal and external stakeholders.

1 Role of the accounting function

The role of the accounting function is to provide information:

- To internal stakeholders through both **financial** and **management accounting** information

- To external stakeholders through **financial** accounting information (published financial statements)

Management accounting provides managers with financial information that they can use to make critical decisions that affect how the company is run.

The accounting function should be set up to ensure that the information it produces is **accurate** and **useful** for both internal and external stakeholders. An organisation can ensure these objectives are met by establishing robust processes and controls. These will enable an organisation's employees to understand exactly what is required of them, and ensure that there is sufficient training, time and resources allocated, so that they can provide this information to the standard required.

2 Stakeholders of organisations

To understand why financial statements are produced, it is important to first consider who the users of the accounts will be. Some reports are used for external reporting purposes, eg statement of profit or loss, and others for internal use only eg budgetary reports.

2.1 Types of stakeholder

Key term

> **Stakeholder** are individuals or groups that, potentially, have an interest in what the company does.

A stakeholder is anyone who is affected by the actions of the organisation.

Stakeholders can be:

- Internal or external to the organisation eg banks (external) and shareholders (internal)
- Directly or indirectly affected by its actions eg customers, suppliers, employees, beneficiaries

2.2 Expectations of stakeholders

Each type of stakeholder has a different role in relation to the organisation, and therefore has different expectations of the organisation.

Stakeholders in business	What is at stake?	What do they typically expect of the business?
Owners (Shareholders or partners or proprietor)	Money invested	A return on their investment so that their wealth increases: • Steady, growing profits paid out by the business • Growth in capital value of their share of the business
Directors/managers	Livelihoods, careers and reputations	Fair and growing remuneration
Employees and trade unions		Career progression Safe working environment Training, Pension
Customers	Their custom The money they spend on products	Products/services that are of good quality and value Fair terms of trade, continuity of supply
Suppliers and other business partners	The items they supply	Fair terms of trade, prompt payment Continuity of custom
Lenders	Money lent	A return on their investment: • Interest • Repayment of capital

Stakeholders in business	What is at stake?	What do they typically expect of the business?
Government and its agencies	National infrastructure used by business The welfare of employees Tax revenue	Reasonable employment and other business practices Steady or rising stream of tax revenue
The local community and the public at large	National infrastructure used by business The welfare of employees	Reasonable employment and other business practices
The natural environment	The environment shared by all	Reasonable environmental and other business practices

The key stakeholders can be mapped on Mendelow's Matrix in terms of:

- How **interested** they are in the organisation's strategy (would they **want** to resist it?)

- How much **power** they have over the organisation's strategy (would they be **able** to resist it?)

Level of interest

	Low	High
Low	A eg Casual labour Action: MINIMAL EFFORT	B eg Core employees Action: KEEP INFORMED
High	C eg Institutional shareholder Action: KEEP SATISFIED	D eg Main suppliers Action: KEY PLAYERS

Power

A stakeholder that has a **high level of interest** in the organisation and also a **high level of power** – for instance, a bank that has given the organisation a large overdraft and is concerned that it is about to be breached – should be regarded as a key player when it comes to giving it the information it seeks. Organisations in this position should make sure that they keep the bank well informed, and perhaps even involved in its decisions eg authorising large items of capital expenditure.

Other stakeholders, with **lower levels of interest and/or power**, should simply be kept informed to the degree required by legislation or contractual requirements eg small shareholders should be sent copies of the annual financial statements and invited to the annual general meeting as required by company law.

2.3 Information needs of internal stakeholders

Internal stakeholders will require different types of information, depending on their role within the organisation. Management and owners will want to know how the organisation is performing, but will not necessarily need to have a detailed view of what payments any given customer has made on their account. Equally, a purchases ledger clerk will need to know which invoices are required to be paid on the next payment run, and so will need a detailed schedule for review on a supplier -by-supplier basis.

Information provided to internal stakeholders is not formalised by regulatory or legal guidance; instead the users will dictate what information they require and how they want this to be presented to ensure the most efficient way of using it for their own needs.

Internal stakeholders may be using the system to ensure that they can perform their jobs correctly. For example, warehouse staff will need to be able to access the inventory system to check availability or location of stock, sales staff will need to be able to access price and available stock information, as well as accounts receivable to ensure that any credit extended to customers is appropriate.

Staff hours are increasingly being logged using computer systems, such as a card swipe system in factories and online timesheets for office-based staff. This is useful information for management as they pay staff for the hours they have worked, but they can also ensure accurate costing of finished goods (labour rates and efficiencies) and job costings (such as solicitors' and accountants' charge out rates).

Activity 1: Internal stakeholders

Using the CCC scenario (which can be found at the back of this Course Book) consider the following list of internal stakeholders. Note down the information which they would specifically require as employees of CCC.

(a) Directors of CCC
(b) Warehouse manager
(c) Operations manager
(d) Payroll clerk

Required

Explain how each of the stakeholders above would use the information they require, and, where appropriate, consider any risks to the business if the information they receive is inaccurate or late.

2.4 Information needs of external stakeholders

External stakeholders will usually require a more formal and standardised reporting format. If the organisation has a bank loan or overdraft, the bank will want to review the financial statements as well as any business forecasts.

Statutory financial reports must be filed with the Registrar of Companies on an annual basis in line with the Companies Act 2006 and appropriate accounting standards and policies.

Activity 2: External stakeholders

You will be required to use the scenario of CCC for this activity.

Required

Using the pre-seen information provided on CCC, identify the key external stakeholders who would require information regularly from the company. Briefly explain why these stakeholders would require this information.

3 External reporting requirements

Financial reports are used by internal and external stakeholders. External reports will generally have to adhere to a set of reporting requirements laid down in company law and presented in accordance with accounting standards. Internal reports can be less formalised and will be set out according to the type and the needs of the individual organisation.

You will have covered the content, legal and regulatory requirements in Level 4 *Financial Statements of Limited Companies*.

3.1 Statutory financial statements

International Financial Reporting Standards ("IFRS Standards") are updated regularly, therefore it is important that any organisation which uses them to compile their financial statements can accurately compile the financial information.

The purpose and importance of statutory financial statements prepared in accordance with the Companies Act 2006 and accounting standards has been covered in *Financial Statements of Limited Companies*. Here is a brief recap of the key purposes:

(a)   To determine whether the organisation has made a profit or a loss

(b)   To demonstrate how well (or otherwise) the directors have exercised their management or 'stewardship' of the company's resources

(c)   To meet the company's statutory requirement to prepare financial statements that show a true and fair view of its financial performance during a period, and its financial position at the end of it

(d)   To help **shareholders** (and potential **new investors**) evaluate how far their capital invested in the company is at risk, and determine the return they should be expecting to compensate them for this risk

(e)   To help **lenders** and **suppliers** determine whether the company will be able to meet its financial commitments as they fall due

The statutory financial statements comprise of the following:

- A **statement of financial position** is a list of all of the assets, liabilities and capital of the business at a particular point in time (the end of the reporting period).

- A **statement of profit or loss** is a summary of the activity of the company during the reporting period (usually a year).

- A **statement of cash flows** is an analysis of how and why the company's cash balance has changed during a reporting period. In addition to the statement of financial position and the statement of profit or loss, it is important for both management and current and potential investors to understand how cash is being utilised by the business.

Activity 3: Financial statements

CCC has a December year end. The pre-seen information has extracts from the previous year's financial statements.

Required

Identify the reports which would be most useful to the external stakeholders identified in Activity 2.

Highlight any potential issues that may arise in respect of these stakeholders using the financial statements and whether any further information will be required by them in addition to the financial statements.

Activity 4: Cash flows

Here is an extract from the cash flow produced by CCC as at 31 December 20X2. It was produced as part of the pack supplied by the external accountants, Bright & Co. The Cookridge brothers are very pleased to have a statement of cash flows; however, they are unsure how to interpret it.

CCC Ltd

Statement of cash flows for the year ended 31 December 20X2

	£	£
Profit before tax		2,000
Add back		
Depreciation for 20X2	7,000	
Increase in inventory	(24,000)	
Increase in receivables	(51,000)	
Increase in payables	47,000	
		(21,000)
Net cash outflow from operating activities		(19,000)
Purchase of non-current assets	(2,000)	
Proceeds from disposal of non-current assets	5,000	
Net cash from investing activities		3,000
Receipt of loan	60,000	
Financing costs	(5,000)	
Net cash inflow from financing activities		55,000
Net change in cash		39,000
Cash brought forward		(74,000)
Cash carried forward		(35,000)

Required

Briefly explain the significance of the key figures in the CCC statement of cash flows as at 31 December 20X2. Use specific examples from the statement to support your answer.

3.2 Tax regulations

Financial statements are not the only external reporting requirement; the local tax authorities will need to ensure that the organisation is paying sufficient tax based on their profits for the period.

The main taxes for organisations are corporation tax and VAT (Value Added Tax). For *Accounting, Systems and Controls,* you will not be asked detailed computational questions, but you will need to understand the reporting implications on the organisation.

HMRC requires most employers to report their payroll deductions on a monthly basis, using Real Time Information ('RTI'). This required organisations to use updated software that could report this information to HMRC online. It also required organisations to report on a more timely basis, placing both technological and staff burdens on businesses, as information was required prior to payments to staff being made, and additional training required of payroll staff.

VAT must be reported electronically for all VAT-registered businesses, again, requiring upgraded software (or even new software in some cases) and additional training time for staff.

3.3 Other government legislation

Pensions legislation has been introduced whereby employers are required to auto-enrol their staff into stakeholder pension schemes. This has resulted in additional financial burdens (pay contributions) and administrative burdens (ensuring all staff are enrolled within the reporting deadlines and submitting the required returns to the Pensions Regulator) on the payroll staff within the finance function.

Money Laundering Regulations require organisations to register with a supervisory authority (such as the AAT) and ensure compliance with the strict reporting criteria. The regulations also require organisations to ensure additional training of staff to identify and prevent the main elements of money laundering or terrorist financing. In particular, the regulations require an organisation to have documented policies, controls and procedures in place to prevent activities related to money laundering.

4 Internal reporting requirements

4.1 Management accounting

Management accounts are not bound by regulation and are intended to meet the needs primarily of the company's management.

The types of management accounting reports are covered in depth in Level 4 *Management Accounting: Decision and Control*.

These include the preparation of information such as:

- Budgets
- Standard costs
- Variance analysis
- Ratio analysis
- Sales figures for products and/or divisions
- Inventory levels
- Profitability reports
- Any other internal information prepared using financial data

Management accounting reports will be used internally by decision makers to help them:

(a) Make decisions on resourcing and resource allocation.

(b) Manage the company's profitability and cash flow, for example, strong accounts receivable and credit control systems will ensure that prompt payment ('settlement') discounts are taken up when available, and creditors are paid on time.

(c) Monitor the controls and review any areas for unusual or unexpected results which may highlight business-critical issues, control issues or potential fraud. This is covered in more detail in Chapter 5.

Organisations should be taking advantage of available tax incentives too. For example, when considering a new large non-current asset to be purchased, what are the capital allowances available, and does this affect the decision to proceed with the purchase?

Management must carefully monitor the spending of government grants to ensure adequate reporting in the financial statements as well as accurate comparison of actuals against budget.

These reports and how management use this information are analysed in more detail later in this Course Book.

5 Other reporting requirements

Aside from profitability and cash flow, organisations are increasingly being assessed by internal and external stakeholders on their ethical and sustainable practices and policies.

There are various ways in which the organisation can report performance and more generally communicate with its stakeholders on these matters.

5.1 Mission statement

Many organisations seek to summarise their main objective and also their purpose, strategy and values by formulating a **mission statement** which briefly outlines a company's main objective, and its purpose, strategy and values.

Mission statements are published for the benefit of employees and other stakeholders of the organisation. There is no standard format, but mission statements should generally be:

- **Brief** – to help ensure they are easy to understand and remember
- **Flexible** – to help accommodate change
- **Distinctive** – to make the organisation stand out

5.2 Corporate social reporting (CSR)

Increasingly, organisations are being assessed on how they are acting as 'good corporate citizens'. **Corporate social responsibility reports** outline the objectives for ensuring the ethical, sustainable and moral aims and achievements of the organisation.

These corporate social reports (CSR) are usually included within the annual report, and discuss their policies in terms of ethical, environmental, charitable and sustainability factors. Larger companies must report on their social and environmental activities and sustainability impact via dedicated CSR statements embedded within their financial statements. However, smaller companies are also publicising their policies to differentiate themselves from competitors. Although the detailed content is outside of the syllabus, you will need to have an understanding of how ethical and sustainability information has an impact on stakeholders.

Real life example: Jaguar Land Rover

Jaguar Land Rover takes its corporate social responsibility reporting very seriously and aims to provide as much information as possible regarding its aims, its results to date and where it sees that it can develop in the future.

- Sustainability report
- Sustainable development policy report
- Environmental reporting (waste, water usage, recycling, emissions)
- Community projects (staff volunteering to assist with local projects)
- 'Building British' and how it supports the local economies
- Sourcing ethically sourced/recycled materials for the manufacturing of new cars (it uses recycled aluminium)

By putting this information in the public domain, Jaguar is aiming to be transparent about how it performs in ethical, environmental and sustainability terms as well as financially as a company.

(Jaguar Land Rover, 2016)

5.3 Sustainability reporting

There are six main responsibilities of the accounting function in regard to upholding the principles of sustainability:

(a) Creating and promoting an ethical culture within the company

    (i) Supporting ethical policies as they are introduced

    (ii) Discouraging and reporting illegal or unethical practices (money laundering, fraud, theft, bribery, non-compliance with regulations, bullying and short-term decision making)

(b) Championing the aims of sustainability within the context of the company's culture and its own policies on sustainability

(c) Evaluating and quantifying reputational and other ethical risks

(d) Taking social, environmental and ethical factors into account when preparing information for decision-making and performance measurement

(e) Promoting sustainable practices in relation to products and services, customers, employees, the workplace, the supply chain, and business functions and processes

(f) Raising awareness of social responsibility

5.4 Ethical reporting

Organisations may also have ethical values, based on the norms and standards of behaviour that their leaders believe will best help them express their identity and achieve their objectives. Often the ethical values of the company are set out in its mission statement.

Setting standards is important as organisations are responsible for their actions and can be held accountable for the effects of their actions on people and society. Often these standards are not legally binding, rather they are guidelines for specific industries to ensure best practice.

As such individual organisations should behave ethically towards any employees, customers, suppliers and communities affected by the decisions and actions that they take.

The Groceries Supply Code of Practice (GSCoP) is not a legal requirement for supermarkets, however, it outlines and makes recommendations upon retailers regarding fair payment times, supply agreements and rules regarding deductions (including marketing, penalties and delays).

Supermarkets which perform poorly are likely to be questioned by shareholders at AGMs, receive bad publicity and potentially lose sales or contracts with suppliers.

Increasingly, large companies are disclosing their ethical treatment of suppliers in their Annual Reports.

Real Life Example

(Source: John Lewis Partnership Annual Report 2018)

In this extract from the John Lewis Partnership Annual Report, Waitrose confirms that it adheres to the GSCoP, and also highlighted that there had been an increase in queries by suppliers. The organisation also states that they have a specific committee to monitor the treatment of suppliers, and so placing emphasis on its importance to John Lewis and Waitrose.

5.5 Integrated reporting

It is clear that many businesses need to report more than just figures and financial results in their annual reports. With over 70% of consumers stating that they will prefer to use the service of more ethical companies, and over a third stating that would be happy to pay more to ensure that the companies they use are ethical ("Accounting for Good", AAT, 2016), it is clear that reporting in a more 'holistic' manner is increasingly important for modern businesses.

Integrated Reporting <IE> is a way of reporting financial, ethical, and sustainable factors, usually including information on the welfare of staff, assistance to the local community and the business's impact on the environment.

You will not be expected to produce an integrated report in your assessment, but you should be aware that this is one of the ways that businesses can report performances, both with financial and non-financial parameters in their annual report.

Activity 5: Ethical and sustainability information

Here are some extracts from the directors' report contained in CCC's financial statements for the year ended 31 December 20X2, together with the company's mission statement.

CCC mission statement

'Our mission is to provide an excellent level of service to all of our customers – and we endeavour to offer our customers a quality product at a competitive price.

We aim to act ethically towards our suppliers, customers and staff, ensuring the best in service and supporting diverse needs and requirements.

The environment is important to us and we aim to recycle wherever possible; we promise to remove all of our packaging from customers' premises, and dispose of this in an environmentally friendly way.'

Extract from the directors' statement as at 31 December 20X2

Turnover has increased year on year, but margins on the sale and fitting of carpets have been affected by challenging market conditions with larger national firms' aggressive price promises affecting what we can demand for our products and services.

We have recently introduced a vinyl reclamation scheme which can recycle the offcuts from vinyl rolls. The company recycles the off cuts into making traffic cones. A small charge is made for this however, this has reduced our non-recyclable waste costs.

Due to a new contract with Umteeko, we are looking to expand our stores across the South coast as this is proving to be a very popular product.

Required

In respect of the extracts provided, identify what information the following stakeholders are most likely to be interested in.

Stakeholder	Information likely to be interested in
Customers	
Suppliers	
Employees	
Investors	

6 Other regulations

There are other forms of regulation that may impact the accounting function, as a result of either UK Acts of Parliament or EU Directives. These include:

- Taxation regulations including VAT, corporation tax and PAYE for employees

- Data Protection Regulations (GDPR from May 2018)

- Equality and Diversity regulations (including the Gender Pay Gap Regulations which came into force in 2017, requiring large employers to publish data on their gender pay gaps on an annual basis)

- Late payment law as set out in the Late Payment of Commercial Debt (Interest) Act 1998

- Fraud Act 2006

- Bribery Act 2010

- The Proceeds of Crime Act 2002

- Public Interest Disclosure Act 1998

- The Money Laundering, Terrorist Financing and Transfer of Funds (Information on the Payer) Regulations 2017 (as amended)

- Industry regulations – almost every industry has regulations that affect how an organisation operates in that particular industry eg how it disposes of its waste

- Health and safety legislation

- Environmental reporting (Non-Financial Reporting Directive 2014 requires certain large companies in the EU to report on emissions and the Companies and Limited Liability Partnerships (Energy and Carbon Report) Regulations 2018 require additional greenhouse gas, energy efficiency and consumption reporting for periods commencing from 1 April 2019).

Therefore, any accounting function must be able to take a wide range of laws and guidelines to ensure that they are reporting accurate and timely information, not just on financial parameters.

Activity 6: Regulations

All organisations will have a variety of regulatory requirements that they must comply with.

Required

Using your knowledge from other modules where applicable, consider each of the scenarios which CCC may be exposed to and consider how the accounting systems and control would be required to be robust to ensure compliance with those regulations.

Complete the table below focusing on the regulations that CCC may be subject to. Draft some points assessing what controls could be put in place to meet regulation in each given scenario.

Scenario	What regulations should be adhered to?	Expected controls required to be in place
CCC has employees and pays them on a weekly and monthly basis.		
CCC charges VAT on its invoices.		
CCC charges interest on invoices paid late.		
CCC is a private limited company exempt from audit.		

Chapter summary

- An organisation has a range of stakeholders: internal (managers, employees and shareholders) and external (bankers, suppliers, customers, government and local community).

- Stakeholders have differing information needs, and it is the role of the accounting function to provide that information.

- The accounting function aims to process transactions so it can provide information to meet stakeholder needs.

- The company's statutory financial statements serve a number of purposes: to identify profit or loss; to demonstrate the directors' stewardship; to comply with statute; to help shareholders evaluate their investment; to help bankers/suppliers determine the company's ability to pay on time; to help government/regulators determine the company's compliance with its regulatory obligations; and to provide information about the company more widely.

- Statutory financial statements comprise statements of: profit or loss; financial position; and cash flows.

- Financial statements are not the only external reporting requirement, the local tax authorities will need to ensure that the organisation is paying sufficient tax based on their profits for the period

- The management accounts provide information to internal stakeholders so that they can make decisions on resourcing and manage the company's profitability and cash flow.

- There are other forms of regulation that may impact the accounting function, as a result of either UK Acts of Parliament or EU Directives.

1: Introduction to the organisation

Keywords

- **Corporate social responsibility reports:** Outline the objectives for ensuring the ethical, sustainable and moral aims and achievements of the organisation

- **Management accounting:** Provides managers with financial information that they can use in order to make critical decisions that affect how the company is run

- **Mission statement:** A statement of a company's main objective, and its purpose, strategy and values

- **Statement of financial position:** A list of all of the assets, liabilities and capital of the business at a particular point in time (the end of the reporting period)

- **Statement of profit or loss:** A summary of the activity of the company during the reporting period (usually a year)

- **Statement of cash flows**: A summary of the main movements in the cash of the organisation

1 **Which legal requirement is required to be met when handling customer data and information? Tick ONE option.**

	✓
Fraud Act 2006	
Companies Act 2006	
Bribery Act 2010	
Data Protection Regulations	

2 **Complete the following statement:**

A statement of cash flows shows receipt of a loan as part of _____ and proceeds from the disposal of non-current assets as part of _____.

Picklist:

financing activities
investing activities
operating activities

3 **Complete the following statement:**

A bank which has lent money to a company is _____ stakeholder of the company.

Picklist:

an internal
an external

4 **Match the management decision to how it may impact the organisation. More than one option may apply in each scenario.**

	Financial ✓	Ethical ✓	Environmental ✓
Improving recycling rates in the factory by 30% year on year			
Changing supplier who can supply the materials 20% cheaper, but with less control over the supply chain			

	Financial ✓	Ethical ✓	Environmental ✓
Installing a carbon capture unit on the main factory costing £2 million			
Introducing a more generous pension scheme for employees			

5 **Complete the following statements:**

The financial statements of a company must be prepared in accordance with

_____.

It is the responsibility of the _____ to ensure that these are completed and filed with _____ to ensure compliance with that law.

Picklist:

accountants
board of directors
Companies Act 2006
financial controller
HM Customs & Revenue
Public Interest Disclosure Act 1998
the Registrar of Companies

6 **Which of the following are not legal requirements for an organisation? Tick TWO options**

	✓
AAT Code of Ethics	
Groceries Supply Code of Practice	
Auto-enrolment for pensions	
Gender pay gap reporting	

The accounting function

2

Learning outcomes

1.1	**Discuss the purpose, structure and organisation of the accounting function**
	• The difference between financial and management accounting
	• Why different types and sizes of organisation or departments within an organisation will require different accounting information and systems
	• The different accounting team staffing structures that will be required by different types or sizes of organisation
1.2	**Discuss the purpose of the key financial reports and their use by a range of stakeholders**
	• The purpose and content of financial information produced for internal use
	• How financial information is used by both internal and external stakeholders
	• The importance of ethical information and sustainability practices to internal and external stakeholders
	• The following types of financial report:
	– Budgetary control reports
1.3	**Examine the impact of relevant regulations affecting the accounting function**
	• Explain how the structure of the accounting function supports compliance with external regulations
1.4	**Demonstrate an understanding of the impact of management information requirements on the accounting function**
	• How organisational requirements will inform the management information system
	• How management information systems should enable the calculation of performance indicators

Assessment context

Assessment of these topics will be included within a number of tasks in the synoptic assessment at Level 4.

Qualification context

Management accounting has been studied at Level 3 and also in *Management Accounting: Budgeting* and *Management Accounting: Decision and Control* at Level 4. Accounting regulations and the preparation of statutory financial statements have been covered in *Financial Statements of Limited Companies* at Level 4.

Business context

All businesses have some form of accounting function, even if some or all of it is outsourced to external providers. How the accounting function is structured and run, and how it uses the accounting system, is of key importance to the company's success.

The culture of an accounting function will be dictated by the size of the organisation, but often the biggest influence is the management style, and this will have an impact of the level of controls, the morale and efficiency of staff.

An accounting function must produce the required management information both accurately and on a timely basis. This information is used by the management team who can then make the necessary organisational decisions in order to ensure the business is run effectively.

Chapter overview

Introduction

In this chapter we look at the accounting function of an organisation and review different approaches to such functions in the context of **structure**.

Many organisations centralise functions such as accounting and even outsource all or some of the role of the accounting function to third parties. We will consider the impact this has on the organisation and its accounting function, and how they operate.

The different needs of varying stakeholders was introduced in Chapter 1. Here, the focus is on the organisation of the accounting function and the differences between **management** and **financial accounting**.

1 Purpose, structure and organisation of the accounting function

The aim of the accounting function is:

- To process all accounting transactions for the company accurately and completely

- To provide information to stakeholders that is correct and up to date

1.1 Organisation

Key term

> **Structure** is how activities, functions and staff are grouped, co-ordinated and managed.

Whatever its legal nature (partnership, company or charity), there are many different possible structures for an organisation.

The structure of an organisation affects how it operates and performs.

The most appropriate structure in a given situation depends upon the organisation, its objectives and strategy, the people involved and the nature of its business.

Structure is often determined by the **size** and **type** of the organisation, rather than by what it needs to be efficient and effective.

1.2 Types of organisation

There are many different types of organisation. You need to be able to recognise why the type of organisation affects how it is structured and how it operates. In turn these factors affect the accounting function, and the accounting and internal control systems, of the organisation.

1.2.1 Profit making organisations

Many organisations (eg companies) are set up to make a profit, so their main objective will be to achieve a level of profit that meets the expectations of the owners (shareholders, partners, sole trader). These organisations will want to know about the financial results and compare them against financial performance targets, eg actual costs against budgeted costs.

1.2.2 Not for profit organisations

Not for profit organisations exist to perform a service or support a group of people to achieve a variety of objectives. These organisations include:

- Charities
- Social enterprises (community interest companies)
- Sports clubs
- 'Friends' societies (arts, schools, hospitals)
- Mutual societies (credit unions)

External regulatory requirements will dictate to a certain degree how formalised the accounting function will be; for example, a small local village hall fundraising club will have a treasurer and a committee, but no formalised financial function. A larger charity like Cancer Research will have the financial reporting infrastructure in place to support its external reporting functions and internal control requirements and to liaise with the various charity shops, online fundraising resources, outreach groups, and so forth.

1.3 Size of organisation

The size of the organisation will also affect how it is structured and what controls are in place to ensure accurate and timely information.

These factors also affect the specific tasks the accounting function performs.

In a **small accounting function**, staff may be organised to perform multiple tasks.

A small organisation which is growing quickly, especially one which may have poor controls in place, is potentially at a higher risk of problems. Rapid business growth, together with an influx of new staff is a key driver for requiring regular reviews of the accounting system. Such organisations may fail to register in time when they reach the VAT threshold, or struggle with increases in payroll and pension reporting requirements, and for even larger organisations, the need for environmental and sustainability reporting.

Activity 1: Multitasking in a small organisation

At CCC, the staff often multitask. Although Stefan's main role is as Accounts Receivable Clerk, due to him currently studying for his AAT exams he is keen to get involved with, and will gladly take on, additional tasks. Currently, he performs the following tasks:

- Opens the post alone
- Collates and banks the cash and cheques received during his lunch hour
- Raises the sales invoices
- Chases payments from customers

Required

Note any issues with one person covering these roles.

In **larger accounting functions** of big organisations, there may be clear sections of the function which perform the different tasks. There may be separate sections for the following:

- **Transaction processing** is maintaining the accounting records: payroll, sales ledger, purchases ledger, cash book and general ledger.

- **Financial accounting** is producing financial statements and other external reports for regulators, including taxation.

- **Management accounting** is producing cost reports, forecasts and budgets, and any other information required by managers to support planning, performance measurement and decision making.

- **Treasury management** is managing the organisation's cash flow and requirements for finance.

 Real life example: Central finance functions

Think about a large retail organisation such as Marks & Spencer or Boots. They have many branches and lots of information on sales, inventory, deliveries and customer orders to collate. Both these companies have central finance functions which allow them to focus on specific areas. For example, Boots has a treasury function which is solely in charge of verifying cash flow, investing excess funds, identifying areas for further funding and advising senior management regarding large investments and their timing. If the treasury function also tried to maintain the sales orders, given the scale of the organisation, this would soon become very muddled.

1.4 Levels of management

A key aspect of organisational structure is how many levels of management there are between the leader of the organisation – the chief executive officer (CEO) or managing director (MD) – and the people doing the work.

The structure can be described as either tall or flat.

A **tall** structure has the following characteristics:

- Many levels of management

- Each manager is only responsible for a small number of staff (a narrow span of control)

- Is hierarchical

A **flat** structure has the following characteristics:

- Few levels of management from the bottom of the organisation to the top

- Each manager may have many staff working for them (this is known as a wide span of control)

Tall organisation   **Flat organisation**

The trend in modern organisation structures is to flatten or de-layer organisational structures, removing whole levels of management.

No single structure is right or wrong; it must fit the organisation type and size, and there are advantages and disadvantages of each.

Activity 2: Tall and flat organisation structures

Per the scenario CCC has a relatively flat structure, comprising of the following:

Required

(a) **What are the advantages of the flat organisation structure for CCC?**

(b) **Consider the impact on the company if CCC added another two layers of management to make the organisation 'taller'. What benefits or issues could arise?**

Real life example: NHS

The NHS is a very large organisation which has many layers of management, so is a good example of a 'tall' structure. It has a wide range of stakeholders, including employees (who range from experienced doctors and surgeons through to porters and cleaners) and external stakeholders (patient groups, fundraising bodies, regulatory bodies).

The advantages of the NHS's tall organisation structure include the following:

- Narrow span of control – making it easier for management to manage their subordinates.

- Clear management structure.

- Clear lines of responsibilities.

- Clear lines of control – essential for patient safety.

- Employees can see a clear career progression ladder, which can feel more achievable.

- This type of structure is suited to larger organisations.

1.5 Culture of the accounting function

The accounting function is not just the accounting system plus the employees who operate it. A key element of any accounting function is the **culture** that exists within it.

Key term

> **Culture** is 'the way we do things around here'. It may be very different from the way a company might ideally want it to be.

Managers and owners set the standard for the accounting function because they operate it on a day-to-day basis, and therefore determine its culture. This is often what makes one company and its accounting function different from another.

The culture of the accounting function may be:

(a) Based on teamwork – where everyone helps each other to ensure all tasks are completed on time and appropriately by the team as a whole.

(b) Based on individualism – where each member of staff sticks to their own roles and responsibilities.

(c) Based on control – where all rules and procedures are adhered to at all times. The control environment at an organisation will impact on how many and how often the levels of management interact with the staff.

(d) Laissez-faire (relaxed) – where controls are informal and trust is an important part of the control framework.

No particular culture is right or wrong, but a certain culture may be inappropriate to the accounting function in question eg a laissez-faire culture in respect of cash is always risky.

The culture of an organisation may change with personnel or technological changes, such as a new managing director or head of department, or a new integrated software system being installed.

1.6 Ethical considerations

You will have been introduced to the ethical aspects of working in your Level 3 *Ethics For Accountants* course. The ethical outlook of a profit seeking company will play a role in formulating the culture of an organisation and the practices its undertakes eg a commitment to minimising carbon emissions will influence its manufacturing and procurement policies. In relation to their work in an accounting function, an accountant is involved in:

(a) **Economic aspects**:

(i) Supporting their company to be profitable

(ii) Looking for ways to improve the efficiency of the accounting function and the company generally

(iii) Considering how the company's profitability can benefit wider society

(b) **Social aspects**:

(i) Supporting policies on corporate governance

(ii) Supporting local businesses when choosing suppliers and paying them on time

(iii) Consulting the local community when making decisions eg investing in existing premises or relocating operations

(c) **Environmental aspects**:

(i) Supporting their company to use less energy, reduce pollution and manage resources and relationships with a view of the long term

(ii) Running the accounting function in a sustainable manner eg not printing emails unless necessary, turning lights off at the end of the day and recycling materials where possible

For a recap on understanding the ethical considerations when reviewing **products and processes**, revisit the Level 4 module *Management Accounting: Budgeting*. *Management Accounting: Budgeting* Chapter 3 covers budgetary control systems, including how budgeting can promote ethical management.

Ethical budgeting ensures that the targets are achievable, yet not too easy, as well as ensuring that the people who are made responsible for those targets have a degree of control. Staff who are appraised on financials outside of their control will become demotivated. Personal motives should be set aside, such as low targets to guarantee bonuses or setting high cost thresholds so that they are not blamed for any overspends.

Key terms to remember from your Budgeting module include:

Budgetary slack is an extra amount of cost built into a budget by budget holders in order to make the targets easier to meet.

Goal congruence is where the goals of individual functions or departments are consistent with the overall goals and strategy of the organisation. Therefore, supporting the budget co-ordination between departments, encouraging team working and aiming to reduce 'silo' thinking between them.

Activity 3: Culture

Consider the two examples stated above of CCC and the NHS.

Required

What key differences would you expect to find between the cultures of the accounting functions within these two organisations?

2 Working practices within the accounting function

Accounting functions within companies can be centralised or decentralised. Some organisations may have limited staff or experience and so look to outsource some activities, such as payroll or debt collection.

2.1 Centralisation of the accounting function

A centralised accounting function is where the accounting tasks are performed at head office, regardless of where the company's other activities are carried out.

All the data is stored at a central location and accounting function staff process it centrally, although this may be by accessing the system from many different locations. All accounting tasks are performed at head office, regardless of where the company's other activities are carried out. All departments in the company are served by this one accounting function.

Staff will be training according to the department and role they work in, and will have acquired highly specialised knowledge, resulting in increased efficiency.

2.2 Decentralised accounting function

In **decentralised accounting functions** the data is stored and processed locally, and perhaps independently by staff at different locations or with different computer networks. There is no link between processes, each being formed independently of the others.

Staff will need to have a broader awareness of what roles they may be working on; sometimes training and actual job roles will vary between sites, eg the Manchester office may have different working practices and even a different culture to the Southend office within the same organisation.

Activity 4: Centralised accounting function

CCC is proposing to open new stores along the South coast. Rather than having several administration offices, they are looking to use their current accounting team to manage their expanded operations.

Required

List the advantages and disadvantages of CCC having a centralised accounting function. Conclude and recommend which system would be better for CCC based upon the information you have been given.

2.3 Outsourcing the accounting function

Many organisations centralise some, or more rarely all, of the tasks carried out by an accounting function and then outsource this work to a third party, often under strict contractual agreements known as service level agreements (SLAs).

Outsourcing is where an organisation arranges for essential, but often routine or specialised, tasks to be carried out by a third party.

Outsourcing of accounting functions is most popular for routine tasks, such as payroll, which:

- Are highly automated
- Rely on information technology for processing
- Require highly specialised and up to date skills, knowledge or technology

An example is the 'buying in' of the specialised knowledge from a payroll bureau, common in many smaller entities. This shares the cost of specialised software and skilled staff across several companies, producing economies of scale and a cheaper service for all customers. Other areas which may be outsourced include legal services, human resource and debt collection.

Activity 5: Outsourcing

Here is some additional information regarding the staff in the accounting department at CCC:

Sonja Douglas (Wages Clerk)

Sonja joined CCC eight months ago. Although Sonja is willing to work some extra hours if required, she does not want to commit herself to any more permanent hours. Sonja gained a qualification in payroll four years ago, but has never progressed any further or taken any other development courses. She currently works two full days a week.

Stefan Kalinowski (Accounts Receivable Clerk)

Stefan was employed one year ago. He works four days a week, and has chosen not to work Fridays. He has been studying for his AAT exams and is currently studying Level 3. He has an excellent academic background, with one of his A Levels being in accountancy. This is his first accountancy-related role.

Margaret Peterson (Accounts Clerk)

Margaret joined the company 18 months ago (application letter on file but no CV). She is employed on a part-time basis of five half days per week. She has 15 years' experience of working in an accounts office, but no formal qualifications. She has limited experience of working with accounting software.

Required

Write brief notes highlighting where CCC could benefit from outsourcing some of its accounting functions.

3 Management information systems (MIS)

Management information is information provided to management to help them with planning, controlling, performance measurement and decision making.

Most of the information produced by the accounting function for both internal and external stakeholders is based on data about the transactions that it has processed over a given period. These are recorded in the accounting system, which we will look at in the next chapter.

However, some of the data comes from the wider **management information system (MIS)** which is the processing of the various information using computers (or computer software) from multiple departments or functions. This is particularly the case when the accounting function is preparing information for its key internal stakeholder, the management of the company.

3.1 Purposes of management information

All companies require management information for a range of purposes including:

- Planning
- Control
- Performance measurement
- Decision making

3.1.1 Planning

To plan effectively managers need information that helps them make decisions about what should and can be done bearing in mind:

- The resources that are available
- Timescales and deadlines imposed
- The likely outcomes under alternative scenarios

3.1.2 Control

To control performance, management need information to assess whether operations are proceeding as planned or whether there is some unexpected deviation from plan. If so they may need to take some form of corrective action.

3.1.3 Performance measurement

Just as individual operations need to be controlled, so overall performance must be measured and reported, in a budgetary control report or a scorecard.

3.1.4 Decision making

Good-quality information should lead to better-informed decisions across the range.

The larger the organisation, the more robust the systems required. Lots of information will need to be processed and then organised in a way which makes it usable by management.

3.2 Types of information

Different types and quantities of information are required by managers for different purposes.

Key term

> **Operational information** is used to ensure that specific tasks are planned and carried out properly within a factory or office. The operational level would deal with cash receipts and payments, bank reconciliations and so forth.
>
> **Tactical information** is used to decide how the resources of the business should be deployed, and to monitor how efficiently they are being used. The tactical level would deal with cash flow forecasts and working capital management.
>
> **Strategic information** is used to (a) plan the objectives of the company and (b) assess whether the objectives are being met in practice.

3.3 Information requirements in different sectors

Here are some typical information requirements of a manufacturing company and a service sector company.

3.3.1 Manufacturing company

Information type	Example(s)	General comment
Strategic	Future demand estimates New product development plans Competitor analysis	The information requirements of commercial companies are influenced by the need to make and monitor profit. Information that contributes to the following measures is important: • Changeover times • Number of common parts • Level of product diversity • Product and process quality
Tactical	Variance analysis Departmental accounts Inventory turnover	
Operational	Production reject rate Materials and labour used Inventory levels	

3.3.2 Service sector company

Information type	Example(s)	General comment
Strategic	Forecast sales growth and market share Profitability Capital structure	Companies are customer and results oriented. As a consequence, the difference between service and other companies' information requirements has decreased. Businesses have realised that most of their activities can be measured, and many can be measured in similar ways regardless of the business sector.
Tactical	Resource utilisation such as average staff time charged out, number of customers per hairdresser Customer satisfaction rating	
Operational	Staff timesheets Customer waiting time Individual customer feedback	

Activity 6: Sector analysis

CCC is a small retail business specialising in carpets and flooring. The management team have a background in this sector.

Consider some of the information that management would need to look at in more detail to help them plan future budgets or amend longer-term plans.

Required

Complete the table below, using information from the pre-seen scenario and considering the sort of information a company would need to have in order to grow and become more successful in their sector.

Information type	Example(s)
Strategic	
Tactical	
Operational	

Chapter summary

- Many organisations eg companies are set up to make a profit, so their main objective will be to achieve a level of profit that meets the expectations of the owners.

- Not for profit organisations will be established to meet a specific need or to provide a service.

- The types of organisation may also be affected by its size. A small charity will have different requirements to a multinational retail business.

- 'The way we do things around here' or the culture of an organisation can affect how it is structured. It may be very different from the way a company might ideally want it to be.

- Sections of a large accounting function are: transaction processing; financial accounting; management accounting and treasury management.

- A major aspect of the accounting function is whether it is centralised, so the same function serves all parts of the company, or decentralised, so different departments etc have their own accounting functions.

- Centralised accounting functions enable the accounting to be completed at one site. This can ensure efficiency in terms of producing information and liaising with other departments. However, it can also mean that the accountants are 'far removed' from the rest of the business.

- Often businesses will outsource repetitive activities or activities requiring a high level of specialism. A smaller organisation is likely to outsource more technical work, such as tax or legal assistance. A larger organisation may outsource more mundane or repetitive tasks such as batch invoice processing.

- Management structures will vary according to the business need and the culture of the organisation. A tall structure will have many layers of management, whilst a flat structure will have fewer levels of management.

- Management information systems (MIS) are designed according to the need of the organisation. These will vary in complexity but essentially all MIS must allow the organisation to effectively plan, control, measure performance and enable decision making.

- The types of management information which are required are strategic, operational and tactical and vary according to industry.

Keywords

- **Centralised accounting function:** All accounting tasks are performed at head office, regardless of where the company's other activities are carried out

- **Financial accounting:** Producing financial statements and other external reports for regulators, including taxation

- **Management information:** Information provided to management to help them with planning, controlling, performance measurement and decision making

- **Management Information System (MIS):** The processing of the various information using computers and computer software from multiple departments or functions

- **Outsourcing:** Where an organisation arranges for essential, but often routine or specialised, tasks to be carried out by a third party

- **Transaction processing:** Maintaining the accounting records: payroll, sales ledger, purchases ledger, cash book and general ledger

- **Treasury management:** Managing the company's cash flows and requirements for finance

Test your learning

1   **Identify the type of information provided in the following management reports.**

Scenario	Type	
Future demand estimations for the next 12 months		▼
Competitor analysis		▼
Failure rate report of a machine used in production		▼
Customer service response times		▼

Picklist:

Operational
Strategic
Tactical

2   **Which of the following statements about the structure of an accounting function is true? Select ONE option.**

	✓
A centralised accounting function has better communication with business units than a decentralised one.	
A decentralised accounting function has more economies of scale compared with a centralised one.	
A centralised accounting function has more economies of scope than a decentralised one.	
A decentralised accounting function is better placed to produce group accounts than a centralised one.	

3   **Complete the following statement:**

A company with many layers of management can be described as having a _____ organisation structure with managers having a _____ span of control.

Picklist:

flat
narrow
tall
wide

4 **Complete the following statement:**

_____ is used to decide how the resources of the business should be deployed, and to monitor how they are being and have been utilised.

Picklist:

Operational information
Strategic information
Tactical information

5 **Complete the following statement:**

Production reject rate is an example of _____ information.

Picklist:

operational
strategic
tactical

6 **Which of the following is LEAST likely to affect the culture of an organisation? Select ONE option.**

	✓
Teamwork	
Managers	
Accounting software	
Control environment	

7 **Which of the following functions or requirements of an organisation CANNOT be outsourced? Select ONE option.**

	✓
The requirement to prepare statutory accounts at the year end	
Preparation of the corporate tax return for the organisation	
Preparation of the payroll for the organisation	
Batch invoice processing for the purchases department in a large organisation	

Accounting systems

3

Learning outcomes

1.1	**Discuss the purpose, structure and organisation of the accounting function** • The importance of accuracy and cost-effectiveness within the accounting system • The importance of ethics and sustainability within the accounting function
1.2	**Discuss the purpose of the key financial reports and their use by a range of stakeholders** • The importance of ethical information and sustainability practices to internal and external stakeholders
3.1	**Examine an organisation's accounting system and its effectiveness** • Identify the varying financial information requirements of stakeholders (payroll, sales accounting, purchases accounting, general ledger, cash-book and costing systems) • Explain how a fully integrated accounting system enables the extraction of information to meet internal and external reporting and monitoring requirements • Identify how an organisation's accounting system can support ethical standards and sustainability practices • Identify weaknesses in accounting systems that impact on cost-effectiveness, reliability and timeliness • Evaluate impact of weaknesses in an accounting system in terms of time, money and reputation
3.2	**Evaluate the underpinning procedures of an accounting system, assessing the impact on the operation of the organisation** • Identify how underpinning procedures in the organisation impact on the operation of the organisation (payroll, authorisation and control of sales, purchases, capital expenditure, overheads, payments and receipts) • Identify how underpinning procedures in the organisation can support ethical standards and sustainability practices • Identify weaknesses in the underpinning procedures and the impact on cost-effectiveness, reliability and timeliness • Evaluate the impact of weaknesses in the underpinning procedures in terms of time, money and reputation

3.4	Examine current and planned methods of operating
	• Explain why accounting systems should be reviewed regularly to ensure they are fit for purpose
	• Identify and review the methods of operating used by an organisation to ensure that they: – are cost-effective – encourage ethical standards – support sustainability principles and practices
	• Evaluate a computerised accounting system's suitability for the specific information needs of the organisation
4.1	Identify changes to the accounting system or parts of the accounting system
	• Identify suitable changes to the accounting system
	• Explain any assumptions made
4.2	Analyse the implications of changes to the accounting system
	• Evaluate the implications of the changes to operating procedures and time spent
	• Review recommendations against ethical and sustainability principles, including social, corporate and environmental issues
4.3	Consider the effects of recommended changes on users of the system
	• Identify the changes that users may be required to make to working practices to comply with changes to statutory and organisational requirements
	• Consider different methods of support that can be given to users of the accounting system to assist them in adapting to the recommended changes

Assessment context

Assessment of these topics will be included within a number of tasks in the synoptic assessment at Level 4.

Qualification context

How the accounting system works, especially the bookkeeping system, is covered at earlier stages of your studies in Level 2 and Level 3, as are the topics of ethics and sustainability.

Business context

The accounting system is operated by the accounting function to produce information for both internal and external stakeholders. Its efficient and cost-effective operation is key to the company's success.

The objective of the accounting system is to provide reliable and timely information in a cost – effective manner. Any accounting system will be subject to a number of controls to prevent and detect errors and potential frauds.

By documenting the system, staff can ensure that they are following the correct procedures, and it will assist when new staff join the organisation and act as a reference guide, especially when tasks are performed infrequently.

Underpinning the accounting system is the adherence to the fundamental values of the AAT *Code of Professional Ethics.*

BPP
LEARNING MEDIA

Chapter overview

Introduction

In this chapter we look at some examples of how accounting systems are structured and consider how they provide information to key stakeholders of the company.

We then consider how to assess whether the accounting systems in place are suitable for the company and whether any improvements could be made to them.

1 Accounting systems

An **accounting system** is one that takes raw data on transactions as its input, processes this, and then produces many outputs to meet the information needs of stakeholders.

Inputs include:

- Raw data from the accounting transactions

- Data from the users, meaning that all users must have training to ensure accurate usage of the system

- Data from management on subjective areas affected by them, such as journals, provisions and aged receivable adjustments

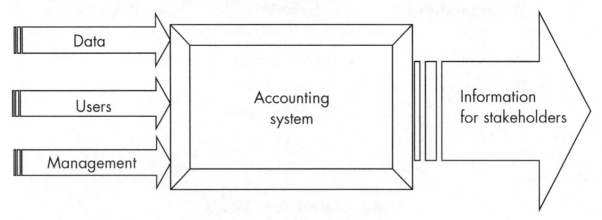

1.1 Objectives of the accounting system

An accounting system is effective if it meets the following objectives:

1.1.1 Cost effectiveness

Cost effectiveness ensures that something is good value.

Key term

Organisations should consider their needs and the complexity of the information they require. The more complex the system, the more expensive it can be to maintain. The cost of training existing staff and new staff on a new or more complex system should be taken into account.

A **large multinational company** will likely have many sites, about which financial information will be required on a timely basis to ensure control. At each of these sites there are likely to be semi-autonomous departments, each having their own specialisms, for instance inventory control, sales orders, purchasing, and preparation of the local management accounts. In large multinational companies of this type it may be necessary to have a dedicated department to prepare and consolidate the accounts for all the overseas subsidiary companies or branches.

In a **small/medium-sized organisation** each department may require its own manager(s) eg purchase manager and sales manager although, in the small organisations, the lines between these managers may be blurred in order to allow holiday and sickness cover.

A **very small organisation** will want to use a more cost-effective, simpler structure, often requiring managers to take on more than one role eg a single person may be in charge of both the sales and accounting functions. These types of entities will often look to outsource more complex areas of the accountancy function, such as using accountants who will prepare payroll, VAT returns and financial statements on their behalf.

Any changes which are proposed to an accounting system should be carefully considered, weighing up the costs and the benefits of making a change. This is covered in more detail in Chapter 5.

1.1.2 Reliability

Key term

Reliability ensures a process or system performs consistently well.

The accounting system must operate effectively, processing all transactions accurately and fully, and must be compliant with applicable laws and regulations. The system should allow access to authorised users only, as and when required, and include data security protocols. A modern system will run regular and automated backups of data. Increasingly companies' data is held offsite 'in the cloud' negating the need for daily, manual backups by users onto discs, USB drives or other hardware.

1.1.3 Timeliness

Key term

Timeliness means that the system should provide information at the required time.

The accounting function and the underlying system needs to be set up in such a way that the reports are accurate and timely. The system will need to provide financial and management information to stakeholders when they require it. It is vital that the system can produce the information required by its users to enable regulatory compliance (such as quarterly VAT returns) and timely reviews of financial performance.

Staff need sufficient training to ensure that they know what information to produce and when it will be required. They also need to have a good understanding of how to use the software to ensure that it is used in an efficient and accurate manner.

2 Accounting system controls

It is vital that an organisation has a strong and robust internal control system.

All systems in the company must be controlled so that they operate efficiently and effectively. Any potential weaknesses in the system need to be mitigated by controls. These **systemic weaknesses** arise within the accounting system itself, which leave it open to fraud and error.

The accounting system must have built-in controls so that it meets:

- Regulations
- The rules and procedures of the company
- The information requirements of internal and external stakeholders

System controls can include:

- Computer controls (such as passwords or restrictions on staff performing certain operations)

- Manual controls (such as internal audit reviews and supervisory checks)

- Physical controls (such as key pads, locking doors, use of safes and removing cash from tills at night)

We will look at detailed examples of internal controls in the accounting system in Chapter 4.

2.1 Documenting the system

Systems control starts at the design phase, during which the data flows and processes are mapped. This forms a template for training the users of the system, so that they understand what the system is doing when they are using it. It is vital that these data flows and processes are documented for future reference, in the event that the system breaks down, or needs updating to ensure that it remains fit for purpose. The detailed controls, monitoring and revisions of the accounting system are covered in the following chapters of this Course Book.

2.1.1 Flowcharts

All information systems work by receiving inputs, then processing these into outputs. Each stage of the process can be analysed in detail to draw up a simple **system flowchart** that clearly shows the flow of data through the system using boxes and text to show the logic.

Completing a system flowchart enables improvements to the system, and thus to the company's processes, to be identified.

Activity 1: Flowchart of credit control

Using the pre-seen information on CCC identify the key elements of the accounts receivable process known at this time.

Required

(a) **Complete a system flowchart for the accounts payable function.**

(b) **Note any gaps in the information which would require further investigation in order to assess the accounting system as it currently stands.**

2.1.2 User manuals

Accounting system controls need to be kept under review to ensure they are appropriate and effective, so that the information output from the system is on time and of the correct quality.

A **user manual** is an accurate analysis of how the accounting system and its controls operate, and how they should be used.

To enable this, the accounting function should maintain an accurate user manual of how the accounting system and its controls operate.

Activity 2: Documentation of controls

CCC Ltd is considering developing a full user manual for its accounting system.

Required

(a) **What are the advantages of the accounting system having a full user manual for all activities that take place within it?**

(b) **What might the disadvantages of such an approach be for an organisation like CCC?**

3 Security of the accounting system

The accounting system must be secured so that it can perform its function. This can be done in a number of ways, for instance preventing initial access to the system with a physical barrier (locks on the doors), or using passwords to prevent unauthorised access to the software.

Physical controls ensure assets such as inventory and cash are safe.

Key term

3.1 Limiting access

All users of a computerised accounting system should have a password that gives them access to the parts of the system they are authorised to use. This ensures staff cannot complete operations that are not related to their role eg access to payroll systems will be strictly limited to HR staff.

Management should guard against malicious or fraudulent access using a variety of **security controls**, such as physical barriers (locks on doors and cabinets), deterrents (alarm system or security), IT controls (passwords, firewalls and ensuring adequate disaster recovery processes are in place, such as backups of data) and monitoring of controls (management reviews, authorisation requirements etc).

Such controls in the accounting system include implementing **integrity controls**, to verify and validate input data, the processing of data and the production of reports.

There should be **application controls** over standing data to ensure only authorised changes are made; for example, new suppliers can only be entered onto a system by an authorised person, or payroll data only accessible by payroll staff.

Ensuring strict **segregation of duties** by reducing the number of people involved in different parts of each process and minimising the opportunity for fraud and error will help to ensure the integrity of standing data and ensuring only authorised transactions are made.

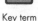

Integrity of data ensures that data is complete, secure and accurate.

Key term

3.2 Preventing errors

The accounting system should have robust integrity controls to verify and validate input data, the processing of data and the production of reports.

These should include input controls on completeness of data input to the system (eg batch processing, total checks, not allowing journals to be posted which do not balance). There can also be programme controls ensuring the accuracy of data input to the system, such as an automatic check on the calculation of VAT. Some controls, such as integrity controls, check the consistency and validity of the data being entered eg the correct format of figures are used (eg allowing invoice numbers in the correct format, AA12345) and checking the calculation of VAT. They are rules in the system which allow only certain types of data to be inserted.

Processing controls verify the data validation and editing procedures. They can also ensure that forms are not closed without being saved or can only be altered by one user at a time. They also used for ensuring arithmetical accuracy or completeness of data. One example of this is 'batch invoice processing' whereby the total value of the invoices is independently calculated and then the total of the invoices entered onto the system is verified against this total.

Activity 3: Security and IT at CCC

Below is an extract from the CCC IT policy currently in place.

> All computers can only be accessed by staff who have been authorised by management to use CCC's computers. All computers must be password protected.
>
> Computers must only be loaded with licensed software owned by the company. No changes to software are permitted without the consent of CCC's directors. No member of staff is allowed to load any software onto computers without prior permission from the management.
>
> No unauthorised devices are to be used for saving, uploading or downloading work (eg discs, memory sticks, external hard drives or other devices) other than those purchased and approved by the company.
>
> Computers should only be used for company business and must not be used to access any social networking sites.

Using the information available in the pre-seen information on CCC, comment on the following.

Required

(a) **What rules should be put in place regarding the use and controls of passwords at CCC?**

(b) **Why are these important?**

(c) **Note any other issues regarding the current security of the accounting system and IT practice at CCC.**

4 Integrated accounting systems

As regulation and reporting requirements become more complex, so the underlying accounting system must also be reviewed and assessed for suitability by management.

The level of complexity and size of the system will depend on the type and size of the organisation.

Large companies produce significant amounts of data and these need to be analysed effectively and accurately. They are likely to require a complex computer system, such as Oracle or SAP, to allow the complex information flows and level of detail required to report to their management and shareholders.

A **small or medium-sized company** will also require accurate reporting information. Using a proven accounting system such as Sage, Net Suite or IRIS ensures that information can be easily passed between departments and allows for management to review the financial position easily.

Sole traders, small partnerships or micro-entities may rely on only one person working part time, and for them more basic software, such as Kash Flow, Sage One or Xero, or even using a basic spreadsheet is sufficient for their needs. Increasingly, these are 'cloud' based to allow the staff and owners access wherever they are in the world. This can be helpful if the sole trader is on holiday as they can still access their accounting function online.

In an **integrated accounting system**, all the data is stored and processed at a central location.

Activity 4: CCC accounting system

Use the information provided about the CCC accounting system in the pre-seen information.

Required

Evaluate the following points:

(a) **The cost effectiveness of the CCC accounting system**
(b) **Its reliability**
(c) **Do management obtain information in a timely manner?**

5 Influences on the system

In previous chapters, we discussed the impact of the organisation's size, culture and type on its accounting function. Here we consider how ethical principles should guide the practices and controls within an accounting system. In the Level 4 module *Financial Statements of Limited Companies* you learned the five **fundamental principles of professional ethics** within the AAT *Code of Professional Ethics* (the AAT Code).

Key term

Integrity is being straightforward and honest in all professional and business relationships.

Objectivity is not allowing bias, conflict of interest or undue influence of others to override professional or business relationships.

Professional competence and due care is having the right level of current professional knowledge and skill to give competent professional service, and acting diligently and in accordance with applicable and professional standards.

Confidentiality is not disclosing confidential information except in appropriate circumstances, and not profiting from confidential information.

Professional behaviour is complying with relevant laws and regulations and not bringing disrepute on the accounting profession.

(AAT, 2017)

Management should ensure that these principles are embedded within the organisation's accounting system.

Fundamental principles of professional ethics are the principles that underpin how a professional accountant should behave.

Assessment focus point

Ensure you have a thorough understanding of the five fundamental principles of professional ethics. If you need to revisit these areas, review your Level 3 *Ethics for Accountants* Course Book for more details.

5.1 Fundamental principles of professional ethics

Ethics is a set of generally accepted principles that guide behaviour.

Key term

Ethical values are assumptions and beliefs about what constitutes 'right' and 'wrong' behaviour. Individuals hold ethical values, often reflecting the beliefs of the families, cultures and educational environments in which they grew up.

Companies should also have ethical values, based on the norms and standards of behaviour that their leaders believe will best help them express their identity and achieve their objectives. The values of the company are usually set out in its mission statement.

Companies, just like individuals, are members of society and are therefore responsible for their actions, and can be held accountable for the effects of those actions eg companies can be convicted of crimes such as manslaughter, just like people.

Therefore, companies should behave ethically towards their stakeholders.

5.2 Ensuring ethical practice within the system

Management and directors need to ensure that ethical practice is maintained within their organisation. Often there will be an organisational policy or mission statement, or a code of conduct that employees are expected to follow.

Activity 5: Ensuring ethical behaviour at work

CCC has recently revised its website, adding information regarding its mission statement (see Chapter 1, Activity 5). Stefan, the Accounts Receivable Clerk, has suggested that the five ethical principles as set out by the AAT *Code of Professional Ethics* be added to the website. The directors have agreed and intend to show how CCC's accounting function (and all other staff) achieves these principles in order to demonstrate what an ethical organisation it is in practice.

Required

Using the table below, identify how CCC can ensure its accounting function (and all other staff) uphold the ethical standards demanded by the AAT *Code of Professional Ethics*.

Fundamental ethical principle	Explain how CCC may demonstrate these principles in practice
Integrity	
Objectivity	
Professional competence and due care	
Confidentiality	
Professional behaviour	

5.3 Ethical risks to the system

The accounting function (Chapter 2) plays an important role in establishing and maintaining the ethical culture within an organisation. Risks to ethical behaviour may come in a variety of forms:

- Criminal behaviour (bribery, money laundering, theft)

- Non-compliance with organisational policy or regulations (data protection, AAT Code)

- Bullying or intimidating behaviour

- Poor decision making (short-term decision making, reputational risks, environmental hazards)

Let us consider some ethical issues concerning CCC's accounting function in line with these fundamental principles.

Activity 6: Ethics conflict at CCC

Consider the following scenarios:

(a) Stefan is asked to produce an aged receivables listing for John Cookridge as at 30 April 20X3. However, he does not have up to date figures because cash received has not yet been allocated to customers, and Stefan knows that the aged receivables report will look worse than the underlying situation. Sonja suggests that to get the report done in time he should use averages for the missing figures.

(b) Margaret has opened a letter from an estate agent requesting financial information about one of CCC's customers, who is applying to rent a property. The information is needed as soon as possible, by email, in order to secure approval for the rent agreement.

(c) A friend tells Stefan on a night out that she expects to inherit money from a recently deceased uncle. She asks him how she will be affected by inheritance tax, capital gains tax and other matters.

(d) A supplier is so pleased with how promptly Stefan paid him that she offers him a free weekend break in a luxury hotel, just as a 'thank you'.

Required

Identify the ethical issues at risk in the scenarios and recommend a course of action to be taken by Stefan or Margaret in each case.

Chapter summary

- The accounting system processes raw data on transactions into outputs to meet the information needs of stakeholders.

- An effective accounting system operates effectively, reports accurately, and complies with applicable laws and regulations.

- Controls in an accounting system allow it to effectively and accurately meet internal and external regulations, and the information needs of stakeholders.

- A user manual documents the accounting system and enables its effectiveness to be kept under review.

- Threats to the accounting system's security include human error, data loss, malicious damage and fraud.

- Security controls include controls over the integrity of data and processing, the system itself, and physical access to the system.

- Using and updating strong passwords are key security controls.

- Flowcharting the accounting system and internal controls enables a systems analyst to see whether controls have been designed effectively.

- The fundamental principles of professional ethics are: integrity; objectivity; professional competence and due care; confidentiality; and professional behaviour.

- The accounting system needs to be operated in an ethical manner, following the five fundamental principles, in order to meet its objectives.

Keywords

- **Accounting system:** A system that takes raw data on transactions as its input, processes this, and then produces many outputs to meet the information needs of stakeholders

- **Application controls:** Controls relating to the transactions and standing data in the computerised accounting system

- **Ethical values:** Assumptions and beliefs about what constitutes 'right' and 'wrong' behaviour

- **Fundamental principles of professional ethics:** The principles that underpin how a professional accountant should behave

- **Integrated accounting system:** All the data is stored and processed at a central location

- **Integrity controls:** To verify and validate input data, the processing of data and the production of reports

- **Physical controls:** Ensuring assets such as inventory and cash are safe

- **Processing controls:** May be used to warn the user if they try to log out before processing is finished or close a document prior to saving. Data is also checked for arithmetical accuracy

- **Security controls:** Controls in the accounting system that cover integrity controls, system controls and physical access controls

- **Segregation of duties:** Making sure that a number of people are involved in different parts of each process to minimise the opportunity for fraud and error

- **System flowchart:** A diagram that shows the flow of the accounting system using boxes and text

- **Systemic weaknesses:** Weaknesses that arise within the accounting system itself, which leave it open to fraud and error

- **User manual:** An accurate analysis of how the accounting system and its controls operate, and how they should be used

Test your learning

1 **Complete the following statement.**

An integrated accounting system is _____. One of its core objectives should be _____.

Picklist:

centralised
compliance with laws and regulations
cost control
decentralised

2 **Identify whether each of the following control activities is an integrity, system or physical access security control.**

Activities	Type of security control	
Validation of input data		▼
Passwords		▼
Archiving		▼

Picklist:

Integrity control
Physical access control
System control

3 **Identify the type of control being demonstrated in the activities below. Select the option from the picklist; some of the options may be used more than once or not at all.**

Activities	Type of security control	
Batch processing of invoices		▼
Only the finance manager can authorise new suppliers on the system		▼
Sequential numbering of invoices		▼
Alerts when the journal being entered does not balance		▼

Picklist:

Completeness
Integrity
Processing
Segregation of duties

4   An accounting system should meet the expectations and requirements of the organisation.

Select the key objectives of the accounting system from the selection below.

Tick ALL that apply.

Activities	✓
Cost effectiveness	
Ease of use	
Reliable	
Providing timely information	

5   **Complete the following statement.**

The requirement for an accountant to act diligently is part of the fundamental principle of _____.

Picklist:

integrity
professional behaviour
professional competence and due care
objectivity

Internal control systems

4

Learning outcomes

2.1	**Discuss how internal controls can support the organisation**
	• Explain the purpose of internal controls
	• Assess how a strong system of internal controls can minimise the risk of loss to an organisation
	• Assess how a strong system of internal controls can ensure ethical standards in an organisation
	• Identify the types of internal controls used in different parts of the accounting function
	• Consider how different types of internal controls suit different types of organisations
2.3	**Examine ways of preventing and detecting fraud and systemic weaknesses**
	• The common types of systemic weaknesses and their causes
	• The need for segregation of duties
	• The role of internal controls in preventing fraud and errors
	• The role of internal controls in detecting fraud and errors
3.2	**Evaluate the underpinning procedures of an accounting system, assessing the impact on the operation of the organisation**
	• Identify how underpinning procedures in the organisation impact on the operation of the organisation (payroll, authorisation and control of sales, purchases, capital expenditure, overheads, payments and receipts)
	• Identify how underpinning procedures in the organisation can support ethical standards and sustainability practices
	• Identify weaknesses in the underpinning procedures and the impact on cost-effectiveness, reliability and timeliness
	• Evaluate the impact of weaknesses in the underpinning procedures in terms of time, money and reputation
4.2	**Analyse the implications of changes to the accounting system**
	• Undertake a SWOT analysis

Assessment context

Assessment of these topics will be included within a number of tasks in the synoptic assessment at Level 4.

Qualification context

How the bookkeeping controls discussed in this chapter operate is covered at both Level 2 and Level 3.

Business context

The internal control system is designed to ensure the company does not fall prey to fraud, error or misstatement of its financial statements. This ensures that the company can operate effectively. The different types of controls within an organisation are identified and explanations as to why they would be important for an accounting system. These are then reviewed in terms of the sales, purchases (including non-current assets) and payroll systems, with activity practice using the CCC scenario.

In this chapter, we look at how a SWOT analysis can be used to identify internal strengths and weaknesses, and external threats and opportunities for an organisation.

Chapter overview

Introduction

In this chapter we define controls further, providing examples of procedures that relate to the meeting of both organisational requirements and statutory ones. We provide examples of activities for three key accounting functions: sales, purchases and payroll.

We then review the aims and objectives of monitoring controls within a company. We look at the assessment of **risk** and how it might affect the integrity of any controls in place. We then cover how to analyse internal controls in the sales, purchases and payroll sections of an accounting system.

Key term

Risk is the threat to the company presented by the control objective not being attained.

1 Internal controls

Internal controls are procedures that address the risk that the aims and objectives of the company will not be met.

The purpose of internal controls is:

- To protect the accounting system from systemic weaknesses, fraudulent activities and human error

- To ensure the accounting system complies with applicable laws and regulations

- To ensure the company is working to meet its objectives

Internal controls work alongside the **control environment** to create the overall control framework. This is known as the **internal control system** and is the combination of the control environment, the risk assessment process, control activities and monitoring of controls.

Robust internal control systems:

- Reduce systemic weaknesses in the accounting system, including the scope for errors

- Reduce the risk of loss or fraud

- Ensure that the accounting system operates appropriately

- Ensure the accounting system can change in line with the environment and organisational requirements

- Ensure that ethical standards are met within an organisation

2 The control environment

The **control environment** is formed by the attitudes, awareness and actions of management and those responsible for ensuring that the internal controls within the company meet that company's needs.

The control environment is part of the internal control system, alongside the internal controls themselves.

The owners or management of a company must ensure that these control activities are **regularly monitored** to ensure that nothing goes wrong. If the controls are not followed and management do nothing in response, then the internal control system will not operate effectively eg if a manager knowingly authorises a fraudulent expense claim by a subordinate, then the internal control requiring expenses to be authorised by management is undermined by the weak control environment.

Management must regularly assess the **existing** system and **identify any new risks** which may affect how robust the control system currently is. Without this monitoring, there is unlikely to be a strong control environment.

Indications of a good control environment include the following:

(a) Management communicate and enforce integrity and ethical behaviour.

(b) Management and staff are well trained and competent.

(c) Management operates in a way that promotes control eg regularly monitoring whether the controls are working and adhered to in practice.

(d) The company and accounting function is structured in a way that promotes control.

(e) Authority and responsibility for controls is assigned to separate people ie segregation of duties is commonplace.

(f) Human resources policies promote controls.

(g) Management regularly review and reassess any new or potential risks to assess whether the controls in place are robust enough to ensure a strong control environment.

3 Types of control activities

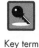

Key term

> **Control activities** are the policies and procedures that help ensure that objectives are carried out.

The types of control activity that should be used in an accounting system to address systemic weaknesses can be remembered using the mnemonic **SPAMSOAP**:

(a) **S**egregation of duties – making sure that a number of people are involved in different parts of each process to minimise the opportunity for fraud and error eg different members of staff should (1) open the post, (2) record cheques received and (3) bank cheques received. These can be built into integrated computer systems, eg an invoice is raised by one user, but a manager must log in to approve them. Others may be manual, such as proof of authorisation by a signature on a hard copy report.

(b) **P**hysical controls – controls over the physical security of accounting records and assets such as cash and inventory eg lock cash receipts in a safe until they are banked; require codes to unlock the cash tills; lock the stores where inventory is kept.

(c) **A**uthorisation (approval) of transactions by supervisors and managers – this shows the person processing the transaction that it is valid, eg overtime should be approved by departmental heads. **Authorisation controls** ensure that only authorised personnel can make changes, such as to standing data or to authorise a bank payment.

(d) **M**anagement controls – managers should review whether activity controls are being carried out within the accounting system eg comparing budget to actual performance in a budgetary control report, and comparing performance and position from one period to the next using ratio analysis.

(e) **S**upervisory controls – there should be close oversight of people performing accounting tasks day to day.

Key term

Reviews are performed by supervisors or managers by looking at summaries and reports of transactions, eg to ensure they are reasonable.

(f) **O**rganisation – the way tasks and the business as a whole are organised should support internal control eg clear lines of responsibility, delegation and reporting, and adequate resources being available for the accounting system.

(g) **A**rithmetic and bookkeeping (often referred to as **accounting controls**) checks on whether transactions have been processed accurately and completely eg **reconciliations** such as a bank statement and a cash book, or a purchases ledger account and a statement from the supplier, can also highlight if errors have occurred. Other accounting controls can be highlighted by a trial balance being out of balance or a computer system not allowing a journal to be posted where the debits do not equal the credits. By using control accounts and trial balances these can help to identify mistakes in the accounting records.

Key term

Reconciliations are checks where staff ensure that two different sources of information agree or that any differences are understood, eg bank reconciliations verifying the bank statement to the bank account on the nominal ledger.

(h) **P**ersonnel controls – appropriately recruited, selected and trained accounting staff should be employed.

Activity 1: The control environment

Consider the following scenario at CCC which occurred in September 20X2:

Stefan was the first to arrive at work on Monday morning. He opened the post, and began logging cash and cheques received into the day book when the telephone

BPP
LEARNING MEDIA

rang. It was Margaret to say that she had an emergency dental appointment for that morning, so she would be late for work. Stefan went back to his task of processing the mail; without noticing he had dropped a cheque behind the desk, before he had written it into the day book. Stefan put the day book, with the cheques inside, onto his desk whilst he went to discuss the morning's deliveries with the warehouse manager.

Paula popped into the office before she joined her husband, John, for lunch. As she was short on cash, and did not have time to go to the bank, she helped herself to £40 from the petty cash tin, and told Stefan that John would replace it this afternoon when he returned from their lunch date.

Paul Collins asked when Pritpal, one of the fitters, would be at work as he needed some rolls of vinyl to be moved into the warehouse from the pallet delivery outside. Pritpal is certified in counter-balance forklift truck operation. In Pritpal's absence Jake Brew offered to move the vinyl as he has been shown how to use the forklift by Pritpal on a number of occasions. Paul accepts his offer as Pritpal is delayed in traffic.

John was concerned that some customers were becoming increasingly slow in making payments on their credit accounts. He asked Stefan to prepare a schedule of receivables, but Stefan was busy drawing up the sales invoices (he uses his Word template and manually inputs details from the sales team) and asked if this could be done next month. Stefan had not chased up late payments recently because he was too busy. Constructing a receivables ledger from the word document invoices took at least two to three hours, and there was a lot of post still to be processed that morning.

Sonja, who had been on holiday, was approached by Ron Sellers, one of the sales team. He had been expecting commission totalling £800 in his wages, but Margaret (who had covered for Sonja last month) had not processed this and had only prepared his wages based on Ron's basic hours worked. Ron told Sonja that he really needed this money, but Sonja, knowing she could do nothing until the next wages run, told Ron he would have to wait seven days.

Ron was so upset by this news that Sonja was consumed with guilt, and she told Ron that she would borrow the money out of the petty cash tin and replace it when she made his wages up next week.

Required

Highlight areas of weakness from the extract above relating to CCC.

4 Sales system controls

The various parts of the accounting system require different internal controls. Here we look at the types of controls that are found in sales systems, and the risks that they are designed to mitigate.

Cash sales are particularly risky, as when a company makes a cash sale no credit is granted. As the customer chooses and pays for goods on the spot, no formal order is raised, resulting in inventory being issued without a sales order form. The risks this poses are discussed later.

In this section, we focus on the correct actions which need to take place to ensure controls are in place. These are the **control objectives** of the credit sales sub-system, and the risks inherent within.

4.1 Controls in the sales system

4.1.1 Segregation of duties

Dividing tasks among several staff members in the sales system, especially in relation to handling cheques and cash receipts, is a key control. By ensuring that one member of staff completes a task, and another reviews the process, it is easier to prevent and detect the following frauds and errors:

(a) **Ghost customers** – creating a false customer who orders goods but does not pay – in effect stealing the company's inventory. This is possible if the same person is in charge of orders and credit control/accounts receivable (sales ledgers). This risk is mitigated by segregation of duties eg new customers are approved by management, then a different employee enters them onto the system following an external credit check.

(b) **Stolen cash receipts** – cash received is not recorded in the ledgers, it is stolen by employees. Alternatively, an employee could intercept cheques when they arrive and steal them before they are recorded. Segregation of duty is operated here by having the person opening the post supervised during the process.

(c) **Overcharging on sales** – goods sold are overcharged, with employees keeping the additional amount received from customers.

(d) **Inflating customer orders** – additional goods are added to a customer's order, but not invoiced to them. Instead, the excess inventory is retained by the employee for their own use, or to sell on privately.

(e) **Writing off debts** – writing off amounts owed when in fact the debt was paid in full. The employee then keeps the written-off amount.

(f) **Raising credit notes** – that are not sent to the customer, who therefore pays in full. When payment is received in full the employee keeps the cash matching the false credit amount.

(g) **Teeming and lading** – allocating one customer's payment to another in order to balance the books and detract from a shortfall.

Key term

Authorisation of transactions is a key control activity, indicating to accounting staff that the transaction in question is valid.

Activity 2: Sales controls (1) – customers and orders

The following describes the procedures which CCC currently uses for accepting new customers, taking sales orders and the delivery process.

While some customers pay cash for their goods, over 60% take credit terms. Customers are granted 28 days to pay their invoice in full, interest free. CCC uses a credit reference agency for orders over £200 to ensure that potential new credit customers have no history of poor payments. Once the agency has done this check, the customer is automatically granted an unlimited line of credit. The sales staff are in charge of calling the credit agency at the time of sale but, as Stefan had recently identified, this does not always happen if junior staff are on duty, or it is a busy day of sales.

All new credit accounts are set up on the first day of the calendar month. All sales orders are received by the showroom store staff for processing, and after completion are passed to the accounting function the next morning, so that Stefan can prepare and record the invoices. Stefan has designed a form in Microsoft Word that he uses as a template for invoicing. All invoices are logged onto an Excel spreadsheet which can be accessed by the accounting team.

The operations manager asks Stefan for a copy of the Excel spreadsheet so he can plan the deliveries for the next week. Once this schedule has been drawn up, the inventory is identified and marked up for delivery. A dispatch note is drawn up and this is handed to the customer. The dispatch note is a manual form which details the customer's address and the invoice reference.

CCC contacts the customers a few days beforehand to agree a delivery time. If the flooring is to be fitted, then the name of the fitter will be supplied. When the flooring has been delivered and fitted, the fitter hands the delivery note to the customer who retains it. The customer does not pay the fitter.

Required

(a) Identify the controls in place at CCC for the sales system; and

(b) Explain the control activities from the control objectives supplied, noting any risks and making any recommendations for improvement.

Control objective	Control activity	Risk and recommendations
Completeness of recording sales.		
Record invoices in the correct time period.		
Only creditworthy customers are offered credit terms.		
Record goods dispatched in the inventory system.		

Activity 3: Sales controls (2) – Credit control

The following information has been obtained as to the cash collection procedures at CCC.

Company credit control policies

The company policy regarding non-payment is as follows:

- Once payment is seven days overdue Stefan will telephone the customer.

- If payment is not received within 14 days of the telephone call, then Stefan writes to the customer requesting payment and for the account to be brought into order.

- If payment is still not received within the next 14 days, the customer's details are passed on to a debt collection agency which works on behalf of the company.

The debt collection agency charges £80 per case, plus 30% of any monies collected. Though this is their policy, the directors rarely bother following it through.

As the invoices are manually input onto Word templates, set up by Stefan, he must create an Excel spreadsheet each month to look at what money is owed. He usually rolls forward the spreadsheet from the previous month, but as he is very busy and management do not prompt him, he sometimes misses a month.

Stefan opens the mail every morning and sorts through it. Any cash or cheques received from customers are entered manually into a day book to record the receipt. The day book is then used to update the ledger accounts, and the cheques and cash are placed in the office safe until a banking day.

At the end of every day, all cash and cheques are removed from the tills, leaving a float of £100 cash in each till for the start of the next day. The principle is that the till should be balanced to ensure that the cash content is correct.

However, during the week this does not happen, and the sales staff feel that they should not be asked to do an extra job after closing. The first salesperson in the next day counts the till contents and takes it upstairs to the accounting office for Stefan to bank it.

As a result, it is common practice that all cash (except for the till floats) and cheques are removed and bagged as takings from individual tills before being stored in the safe in the accounting function office.

Banking

Banking is carried out on Monday and Thursday, and this is normally Stefan's job, which he does during his lunch break.

Recently, available cash from the office safe has been used to pay wages in order to reduce the amount of money drawn from the bank via cheques.

Required

(a) Identify the controls in place at CCC for credit control and cash collection.

(b) Explain the control objectives and activities, noting any risks and making any recommendations for improvement.

Control objective	Control activity	Risk and recommendations
Record all invoiced sales in the accounting records (sales ledger and general ledger).		
Record invoiced sales in the correct sales ledger accounts.		
Identify debts for which payment might be doubtful.		
Record all money received.		

Control objective	Control activity	Risk and recommendations
Bank all money received.		
Safeguard money received until it is banked.		

5 Purchases system controls

The purchases system – from placing an order to paying the supplier's invoice – is a part of the accounting system which it is particularly important to have controls over because:

(a) The purchases system involves receiving inventory and paying cash – arguably the two types of asset which are most open to fraud and theft.

(b) Purchases may be of very high value, particularly when the company is incurring capital expenditure.

(c) Information from the purchases system becomes part of the data which supports the costing system. Errors and fraud in purchasing will lead to inaccurate information being used for planning, decision making and performance measurement.

(d) The purchase of inventory will affect any manufacturing or retail process. If the information is not accurate, there is a risk of delays to the manufacturing process or delays in fulfilling orders from customers.

5.1 Controls in the purchases system

5.1.1 Segregation of duties

Once again segregation of duties is vital. The chief concern is that a person could order and pay for personal goods through the company, so ordering and payment should be separated.

The risk of fraud will also be reduced if the person who authorises invoices for payments is independent of the person clearing the payment itself.

5.1.2 Authorisation

All purchases should be authorised, however, it would be impractical to have one person authorise every item of expenditure, especially if it required often and in large quantities. To mitigate for this, accounting systems often have set levels of approval for regular purchases, with monitoring controls by management to check over the weekly or monthly expenditure reports. Often there will be maximum amount which will then require management approval, such as £10,000 for a line manager and £50,000 for a supervisor.

Activity 4: Purchases system controls

Here is a summary of the CCC purchases control system:

All inventory is purchased on credit terms from a very wide range of suppliers. This is one of Peter's roles, and he enjoys spending time researching new inventory lines. He also likes meeting the sales staff from different suppliers. He has a favourite group of suppliers he tends to use, mainly because they are sometimes willing to sponsor his motorbike and racing efforts. There is no formal list of suppliers.

Margaret has worked on Excel previously, but this was over ten years ago. While she is competent at inputting data she sometimes struggles with anything beyond this.

Inventory is ordered by Margaret, who receives the request from the warehouse staff, often verbally, especially if the customer needs the goods urgently. The larger suppliers do provide next-day delivery, which is very useful for CCC.

When the inventory arrives in the warehouse, it is signed for by whomever is available in the warehouse. They should check for any damage, but time is at a premium, and most of the junior staff will accept any delivery, and move it to a space in the store. The goods received note (GRN) is put in the in-tray and is taken up to the accounts department when the tray gets full, which is usually once a week.

Margaret will input the invoices she receives (Stefan opens the post and will bring any invoices into the office that same morning) onto the Excel spreadsheet, detailing the following:

- Supplier name
- Description of the item purchased (including dimensions)
- Cost price

If Margaret has a GRN which matches an invoice, she will clip them together and file them away. She uses her Excel spreadsheet as the basis for running the end of month supplier pay run.

Suppliers are paid at the end of the month in which their invoice is received, as long as funds are available. However, some suppliers now request payment within 30 days of the date of invoice, and this is beginning to cause John some concern.

CCC holds a large inventory, with many rolls (often older or discontinued ranges) of carpet in the warehouse for sale on a cash basis.

All suppliers are paid by cheque. These are completed by Margaret, and then signed by either John or Peter as they are now the only authorised signatories. The cheque book is stored in a locked drawer in Margaret's desk in the accounting function office. Occasionally, when the brothers are away from the office for a few days they pre-sign some cheques so that Margaret can make any emergency payments in their absence.

Required

(a) **Note FOUR key weaknesses in the CCC purchase and inventory system.**

(b) **Highlight the risk and propose a suitable control to be implemented by management.**

Weakness	Control proposed	Risk controlled

Weakness	Control proposed	Risk controlled

5.2 Non-current assets

Generally non-current assets purchases are less frequent purchases for an organisation, but the same rules apply in that the expenditure should be authorised.

An organisation will have established rules regarding the purchase of non-current assets, which may look something like this:

Generally the budget for a new non-current asset will be approved by a member of the management team, but sometimes, in larger organisations there may be a Budget Committee who will make large, financial decisions. In both cases, a business case together with initial expenditure, estimated payback and useful life will be part of the report submitted for approval.

Increasingly, organisations will want to see what the tax implications would be on such large purchases, eg what are the capital allowances, are there any grants available, maybe the land to be developed is in an area which attracts government funding.

The organisation is likely to have an approved list of suppliers, and several quotations will be obtained to ensure the most suitable price and terms and conditions of purchase.

The payment to be authorised will be agreed against the budgeted figure, and any discrepancies investigated.

6 Payroll system controls

Payroll is a high-risk area, with the segregation of duties and a review of the amounts to be paid mandatory to ensure a robust control environment. Risks are increased if the payroll is run manually and cash is the main basis for payment to staff.

Activity 5: CCC – Payroll controls

Here is some information regarding the payroll system at CCC.

Until six months ago the payroll was completed by the company's accountants, Southampton Accounting Services. Sonja now runs the payroll on a weekly and monthly basis.

The warehouse, delivery and fitting staff are paid weekly in cash. Pay packets are available from the Showroom Manager, Jim Andrews, from 10:00 am on a Friday morning.

The rest of the staff are paid monthly, by BACS, on the last working day of each month.

Sales staff earn a commission of 2% on the first £7,500 of sales per month, and 5% on any sales over that figure. John Cookridge is responsible for preparing staff rotas to ensure that there is adequate staff coverage for all opening hours. Most of the sales staff are willing to work overtime, so this does not usually create any problems.

Fitters are assigned to their respective duties on a weekly basis and are usually notified on a Monday morning when they arrive at work.

Once the week has finished, the completed rotas are given to Sonja, who uses them to calculate the amount of hours that the individual employees have worked.

Sonja prepares the payslips from this information on a Wednesday, calculating manually any overtime payments due and any Sunday working. From this, she calculates how much cash needs to be drawn from the bank and uses the company cheque book (which is kept locked in Margaret's desk) to prepare a cheque ready for signing.

On a Thursday she prepares the pay packets, which are stored in the office safe for the Showroom Manager to collect and hand out to the staff the following day, though any member of sales staff who is not busy will actually do this. Any pay packets not given out are returned to the office safe by Sonja and remain there until collected by the relevant member of staff.

Salaried staff are paid monthly on the last working day of the month, and this is done using BACS. The BACS information is prepared by Sonja, signed by either of the directors, and needs to be with the bank by the 25th of each month. The directors will check the salaried staff payments to Sonja's calculation schedule. Sonja can input the details onto the bank system for the payments and can authorise the payments up to a value of £10,000 per BACS run. This is adequate to cover the salaried staff, except if the commissions are high or at Christmas. Then the BACS run must be further authorised on the banking software by one of the authorised signatories. No further checks are made by the directors.

Envelopes with payslips are handed to each member of the salaried staff by Sonja on the day they are paid. If a staff member is not available, the envelope is placed in their desk drawer.

There is no requirement, or system in place, for either store or office employees to sign in or out when they start or finish work.

Required

(a) **Document the payroll controls currently in place at CCC.**

(b) **Consider where any control weaknesses lie, and what control activities should be introduced to mitigate risks to the company.**

Payroll control in place	Control weakness	Suggested control to be introduced

Assessment focus point

The activities in this chapter are to enable you to practise identifying the key risks, weaknesses and controls in place in different systems. In the exam, you may be asked specific questions regarding controls over trade receivables (consider the sales cycle), inventory and work in progress (think about purchases controls). Consider also the differences between service, manufacturing and retail industries.

7 SWOT analysis

A useful tool for analysing the control system, as part of the **risk assessment process**, is a **SWOT analysis**. SWOT stands for:

- **S**trengths
- **W**eaknesses
- **O**pportunities
- **T**hreats

The strengths and weaknesses of a system will be **internal** factors.

Once strengths and weaknesses have been identified then recommendations can be made to address the weaknesses.

Opportunities and threats are **external** to the actual system itself.

In these instances, management need to consider how they can use these external opportunities (such as market conditions) or mitigate against potential threats (eg changes in legislation, interest rate changes).

A SWOT analysis is a way for management to highlight the key issues; however, it is important that they focus on only a few at a time as proposing too many changes may be detrimental to staff morale, confusing to customers or clients, or expensive to implement in terms of time and financial outlay.

Key term

A **risk assessment process** is an evaluation of the risks to the achievement of objectives.

Use the information received in the pre-seen information and this chapter in respect of CCC.

Required

Complete a SWOT analysis for CCC using the format below, focusing on the strengths and weaknesses of the internal accounting systems, and the opportunities and threats for the company as a whole.

Strength	Weaknesses

Opportunities	Threats

7.1 Limitations of internal control systems

The inherent limitations of the effectiveness of internal controls include:

- People make mistakes that may not be picked up by software or human review.

- People may not operate controls properly, thus negating them.

- People may deliberately circumvent control systems if they want to defraud the company.

- Lack of review of the controls in place mean that there is no incentive for staff to follow them.

- An overreliance on controls, especially computerised controls, can breed complacency meaning they go undetected.

Assessment focus point

If you are asked in the assessment to consider the limitations of controls, ensure you have read the scenario carefully to ensure your answer is tailored to the question, eg in the case of CCC there appears to be little or no regular review of the controls. Stefan is asked about the aged receivables ledger when cash flow becomes an issue rather than on a regular, monthly timetable.

Chapter summary

- Internal controls in the accounting system aim: to protect it from systemic weaknesses; avoid fraudulent activities and human error; ensure compliance with applicable laws and regulations; and ensure the company is working to meet its objectives.

- The internal control system consists of: an effective control environment; a robust risk assessment process; appropriate control activities; and consistent monitoring of controls.

- Control activities in an accounting system address systemic weaknesses and control risks.

- Control activities consist of: segregation of duties; physical controls; authorisation of transactions; management controls; supervisory controls; organisation; arithmetic and bookkeeping controls; and personnel controls. The SPAMSOAP mnemonic may help you remember these.

- Application IT controls affect transactions and consist of: input controls; accuracy controls; authorisation checks; processing controls; and controls over standing data.

- General IT controls protect the general computer environment.

- The limitations of controls include people making mistakes, where controls may not be operated effectively or where people may deliberately circumvent controls.

- For each control objective within a sub-system, the risks controlled and control activities need to be identified.

- Within any of the sub-systems, segregation of duties – as far as it is possible given the size of the accounting function and the number of its staff – is a vital control.

- In the credit sales sub-system, control objectives etc are identified for: taking orders and extending credit; dispatching and invoicing goods; recording and accounting for sales and returns; and receiving payment.

- In the purchases sub-system, control objectives etc are identified for: ordering; receipt of goods and services; accounting; and payments.

- In the payroll sub-system, control objectives etc are identified for: setting wages and salaries; recording; payments; and deductions.

Keywords

- **Accounting controls:** Control accounts and trial balances which help to identify mistakes in the accounting records

- **Authorisation controls:** A key control activity, indicating to accounting staff that the transaction in question is valid

- **Authorisation of transactions:** These ensure that only authorised personnel can make changes, such as to standing data or to authorise a bank payment

- **Control activities:** The policies and procedures that help ensure objectives are carried out

- **Control environment:** The attitudes, awareness and actions of management and those responsible for ensuring that the internal controls within the company meet that company's needs

- **Internal controls:** Procedures that address the risk that the aims and objectives of the company will not be met

- **Internal control system:** The control environment, the risk assessment process, control activities and monitoring of controls

- **SWOT analysis:** A way for management to highlight the key issues, and review where the organisation has strengths and weaknesses and to consider any opportunities or threats from internal and external sources

1 **What type of control activity is each of the following actions?**

Action	Type of control activity
Person A matches dispatch notes to invoices; Person B creates invoice to customer	
Control account reconciliation	
Petty cash box kept locked	
Adequate resourcing of accounting function	
Review of budgetary control report	

2 **Complete the following statement:**

In SWOT analysis, strengths and weaknesses are _____ and opportunities and threats are _____.

Picklist:

external to the company
internal to the company

3 **Complete the following statement:**

Management should regularly ensure that staff perform _____ of the sales ledger to ensure accuracy and completeness of the data.

Picklist:

assessments
inspections
reconciliations
teeming and lading

4 **Complete the following statement:**

Control objectives in relation to taking orders and extending credit are part of the _____ sub-system of the accounting system.

Picklist:

payroll
purchases
sales

5 **Complete the following statement:**

Completion of GRNs is a control activity related to the control objective of

_____.

Picklist:

ensuring goods and services received are used for the company's purposes

only accepting goods and services that have been ordered and appropriately authorised

only accepting goods received that are of a sufficient quantity for the purposes of the organisation

recording all money received

6 **Complete the following statement:**

Allocating one customer's payment to another in order to balance the books and detract from a shortfall is called _____.

Picklist:

identity fraud
inflation
reconciliation and review
teeming and lading

Learning outcomes

2.2	Evaluate how information from the organisation's financial statements may indicate weaknesses in its internal controls
	• Use ratio analysis
	• Use key performance indicators
2.3	Examine ways of preventing and detecting fraud and systemic weaknesses
	• The common types of fraud
	• The common types of systemic weaknesses and their causes
	• The need for segregation of duties
	• The financial and non-financial implications for an organisation if fraud occurs
	• The role of internal controls in preventing fraud and errors
	• The role of internal controls in detecting fraud and errors
3.3	Evaluate the risk of fraud arising from weaknesses in the internal control system
	• Identify the impact of a poor internal control system on the exposure to risk for an organisation
	• Grade the risk of fraud using either 'low', 'medium' or 'high' or a numerical grade where the number increases in size as the risk becomes more serious
4.3	Consider the effects of recommended changes on users of the system
	• Identify the changes that users may be required to make to working practices to comply with changes to statutory and organisational requirements
	• Consider different methods of support that can be given to users of the accounting system to assist them in adapting to the recommended changes

Assessment context

Assessment of these topics will be included within a number of tasks in the synoptic assessment at Level 4.

Qualification context

Ratio analysis and the use of key performance indicators are covered in the other mandatory units at Level 4.

Business context

Every company's accounting system is at risk of fraud and error even if the risks never actually materialise. A company with systemic weaknesses in its accounting system and internal control system is particularly at risk. It can lead to serious losses and fines for the company, criminal prosecutions of those responsible, and ultimately the collapse of the company.

Management should assess the risk of fraud and misstatement for each area of the organisation, and here we see how fraud can be graded using a fraud matrix. This grading gives the management team guidance on areas where they should prioritise their resources. The use of Key Performance Indicators (KPIs) both within the context of the organisation and the industry in which they operate, act as useful tools to highlight potential problems areas.

The definition of fraud, and what it can mean to an organisation is covered, together with the impact of fraud on a business.

Chapter overview

Introduction

In this chapter we look at the importance of monitoring controls, and why this should be completed on a continual basis.

Organisations need to have good internal controls to prevent **fraud** taking place, with particular focus on the importance of the segregation of duties within the accounting function.

Management should revisit their controls on a regular basis, checking that the processes designed are actually in place, and that they are being adhered to. We will see how a **fraud matrix** can help to evaluate the risks a company faces. We will then look at how to grade the **risk of fraud**.

Accounting systems are at risk of specific frauds, namely payroll fraud, purchases ledger fraud and sales ledger fraud. We will look at the controls that should be in place to prevent these.

We then look at the effect that fraud might have on a company, together with the action a company needs to take to **detect** fraudulent behaviour, and what should be done upon the discovery of a fraud.

1 Monitoring controls

Controls must be monitored to assess their effectiveness over time.

This review is usually overseen by management or, in larger organisations, an independent internal audit team. Internal auditors will review controls across different departments within the company. The role of internal audit differs from that of the external audit. The external auditors review the year-end financial statements, and give an opinion as to whether the statements represent a true and fair view of the company. Occasionally both sets of auditors will work alongside each other, such as when the external auditors are assessing the controls within an IT system. However, it is important to note that whilst internal auditors are employed by the organisation, the external auditors are not. External auditors are typically engaged to assess the financial records on behalf of a company's shareholders for legal compliance purposes.

In smaller organisations effective monitoring can take place, formally or informally, by function heads. For example, the sales director is likely to become aware of control deficiencies in the sales cycle, as they are responsible for managing the sales department's ongoing performance, so will investigate any reasons behind poor performance.

2 What is fraud?

You were introduced to the concept of fraud and the regulations surrounding it during the Level 3 *Ethics for Accountants* module. It is useful to review the key points before attempting the activities in this section.

Key term

Fraud is a crime in which the criminal intentionally makes a gain or causes a loss to another person by depriving them of assets.

Legally there are three types of fraud (Fraud Act 2006:s.1):

- False representation
- Failure to disclose information
- Abuse of position

With respect to the accounting system the types of fraud which are important are:

- **Misappropriation of assets** which is theft, teeming and lading, payment of false employees or suppliers.

- **Misstatement of the financial statements** which is the overstatement of assets or profit, or the understatement of profit, losses or liabilities.

An accounting system is more open to fraud if it contains systemic weaknesses, making it easy to misappropriate assets, or misstate financial information.

Examples of fraud include, but are not restricted to:

- Falsifying financial statements or documents, such as invoices
- Incorrect accounting to purposely hide debts or overstate profits
- False claims about the products being sold by the company (for example, Silicon Valley start-up Theranos)
- Payment fraud, including teeming and lading (misallocation of cash payments)
- Tax evasion, such as understatement of VAT, PAYE or corporate tax.
- Money laundering
- Insider trading
- Embezzlement (fraud by employees in positions of power or trust within a business), such as by creating fictitious suppliers or employees

Activity 1: Potential frauds at CCC

Using the information obtained about CCC from the pre-seen information and the review of the controls in Chapter 4, consider the key areas where fraud may occur within the business.

Required

Identify the possible frauds that could occur within CCC – even if the controls currently in place make such a fraud unlikely.

	Potential fraud
Purchases and inventory system	
Payroll system	
Bank and cash system	
Sales and aged receivables system	

3 Impact of fraud

Fraud has the following types of impact on a company:

(a) **Financial** – loss of funds or other assets. This in turn affects the company's profitability and the owner's investment in it. It can also affect the company's share price.

(b) **Reputation** – exposure to fraud can affect the company's reputation in the eyes of internal and external stakeholders. This in turn could lead to a loss of business.

(c) **Employee morale** – the trust of existing employees could be damaged. Future recruitment and retention of staff might also be affected.

 Real life examples

The following examples illustrate the financial and reputational impacts upon companies which have been fined for financial misstatement, or not having sufficient fraud prevention controls in place:

Example 1 – Tesco Stores

In March 2017, Tesco Stores was fined £129 million by the Serious Fraud Office (SFO) and ordered to set up an £85 million compensatory scheme for shareholders and bondholders who bought shares between the results announcement and the accounting misstatement being made public. Tesco settled out of court regarding charges of false accounting and misstatement of profits.

The impact on the company was a £214 million cash outflow, not including legal costs, with Tesco recording an exceptional charge of £235 million for the 2016/2017 accounting year end.

(Reuters, 2017)

Example 2 – Rolls-Royce PLC

Rolls-Royce PLC was fined £497.5 million by the SFO in January 2017 in respect of 12 counts of conspiracy to corrupt, false accounting and failure to prevent bribery over a period of 30 years. In addition, the company was fined $170 million by to the US Department of Justice and $25 million by the Brazilian authorities.

(SFO, 2017)

Example 3 – Standard Chartered Bank

The Financial Conduct Authority (FCA) fined the bank £102.2 million for failing to maintain adequate anti-money laundering controls between November 2010 and January 2013.

(FCA, 2019)

4 Controls to prevent fraud and systemic weaknesses

In this section, we look specifically at the types of fraud which can occur within the business and, using the scenario of CCC, identify potential issues and consider the impact on CCC.

The management of a company have a duty to put in place adequate controls to safeguard the company and its assets. You have seen many of the safeguarding controls in the Level 3 *Ethics for Accountants* module, and have also covered them in Chapter 4 (SPAMSOAP).

As we saw in Chapter 4 (Section 3), the main types of controls which can help prevent fraud include controls for the accounting system can be grouped into the following categories:

- **Staff controls** – segregation of duties
- **Management controls** – review of controls and regular checks on control activities
- **Physical controls** – locking away confidential files and ensuring office security
- **Application and general computer controls** – password protection, access limitations and integration of systems

Fraud controls are internal controls specifically against fraud in the areas of staff controls, management controls, physical controls and IT controls.

4.1 Sales system

Fraud within the sales system is possible because the system involves the receipt of money, and this risk is more severe where this is in the form of cash, such as a shop.

Activity 2: Sales system fraud

Here is some further information given about an event in January 20X3 at CCC. Use this additional information and any existing knowledge about CCC to formulate your answer. If necessary, revisit the controls documented in Chapter 4.

Stefan was tidying up in the office one evening, and was surprised to discover two cheques behind a desk. One was dated August, and one November. He put them in the in-tray intending to bank them the next day.

John Cookridge asked for a copy of the aged receivables report, as he hadn't seen one for nearly four months. He was annoyed when he discovered that one of the credit accounts, opened for B. Braithwaite, had made no payments against credit given at all so far. This customer had bought £1,000 worth of goods and paid an initial deposit in July but had made no payment since then. He asked Stefan to track back through the account and Stefan realised that no credit reference agency had been used, so he decided to contact the agency to check on this customer, only to find that he had a very poor credit score.

Meanwhile John continued to review the aged receivables and discovered that not only had debts been written off without his knowledge but also that over 50% of the invoices over 60 days old had no payments allocated against them. Unallocated cash amounted to £5,645.

Stefan advised that there had been a large debt of £2,300 written off the previous month, as it dated back to the previous October. Stefan said that although he had tried to chase the debt, the telephone number rang out, and the customer had taken the flooring with him (so no delivery address had been logged by the sales staff).

When John came to lock up the business at the end of Thursday, he discovered that the tills on the shop floor had not been emptied or reconciled to the day's takings.

Required

(a) **Identify the types of fraud which could occur in the sales system at CCC based on the information you have been given in this extract.**

Fraud which could occur at CCC	Why this risk has arisen

(b) **Consider the financial and non-financial impacts these frauds could have on CCC.**

4.2 Purchases system fraud

Fraud within the purchases system is possible because the system includes the ability to order goods from suppliers and then to make payments.

One of the general controls in place to prevent such examples of fraud is segregation of duties: the same member of the accounting team should not be allowed to place orders with suppliers, book in goods received, and then process payments to them.

Activity 3: Purchases system fraud

The following events happened at CCC during March 20X3.

Margaret needed to place a stationery order for CCC. She asked the staff what they needed and placed the order, including some additional paper for her nephew who is studying at university.

CarPet Suppliers, one of CCC's major suppliers, has requested urgent payment of an invoice that has been outstanding for 60 days. This invoice is for £15,000 and, though this would normally have been paid, there were not enough funds in the bank to cover this amount.

When Margaret informed John of this, he was very surprised at the size of the invoice, and asked her to review all the GRNs for October to see what carpets had been ordered to cause such a large invoice. Margaret spent a day completing this reconciliation and found that there was an error and they had been charged for 1,000 metres of twisted Wilton instead of 100, this having a wholesale price of £15.00 per metre including VAT.

When John was checking the invoice, he asked Margaret to produce a report of outstanding invoices and discovered some new suppliers with long outstanding debts who he did not recognise.

Required

Identify the risks from the control weaknesses in the above extract, and make any recommendations to improve the controls.

Ensure your answer is specific to the scenario.

5 The risk assessment process

As discussed earlier, management should regularly review the controls that are in place. Any review should include an assessment of any new risks, internal (such as a new computer system or management restructure) and external (increased market competition, issues with suppliers etc), that may impact the organisation. In doing so any review should assess the ability of the internal control system to respond to the risk that:

(a) Objectives might not be met – including the company's sustainability and corporate social reporting (CSR) objectives (eg sales targets, waste disposal, staff training requirements and recruitment concerns).

(b) The company may be the victim of loss or fraud – this may be accidental or intended, and arise from internal or external sources.

(c) The system may contain errors that result in misstatement in the financial statements – eg assets overvalued and/or liabilities understated.

(d) The company is engaged in unethical behaviour – either intentionally (eg due to pressures to achieve unrealistic sales targets) or unintentionally (eg poorly trained staff taking on new tasks).

(e) The company fails to comply with its legal obligations – such as non-compliance with company law or health and safety regulations.

The risk assessment process must be robust to reduce or avoid these risks. The main aim of analysing the **risk of fraud** is assessing the likelihood on the fraud occurring and its impact if it does occur, and seeking out ways to minimise the risk.

Activity 4: Payroll risks

Here is some additional information on CCC regarding an event during October 20X2. You may also wish to refer to the payroll information given in Chapter 4.

Sonja, the payroll clerk, was approached once again by Ron Sellers, one of the sales team. He had been expecting commission totalling £1,200 in his wages for October, but complained to Sonja that this had not correctly calculated and subsequently he had been underpaid. Ron was cross and aggressively told Sonja that he really needed the missing money right now.

Sonja was so upset by this that she told Ron that she would borrow the money out of the petty cash tin and replace it when she made his wages up. Ron calmed down and said he would collect it from her at the end of the day, and stated that he hoped it 'wouldn't happen again'.

Joe Bloggins spoke to Sonja and explained that he had taken on an extra member of staff for the Christmas rush and January sales. Joe said that the new employee would be paid on an hourly basis, and that as he was a student he would not pay tax, and could be paid weekly – in cash. Sonja asked for the new starter document that all new employees had to complete, but Joe insisted this was not necessary for temporary staff, and insisted Sonja just add him to the payroll system. Joe said that he would send through the completed document later in the week. Sonja agreed, and added the new worker Andrew Lias to the payroll, leaving herself a diary note to ask Joe for the documentation the next week if it was still outstanding.

Sonja's day was made even worse by the printer jamming, resulting in several of the payslips being printed upside down. Sonja was so fed up, she screwed the partially torn and smudged payslips into a ball and threw them in the bin, assured the directors that she would re-run the payslips first thing the next day, and went home early.

Required

Prepare a risk assessment summary for the payroll system for the directors of CCC. Highlight the key issues which have occurred in the payroll system during October and what regulatory and ethical risks these pose to the organisation.

To: The Directors of CCC
Risk assessment of the payroll system based on events in October 20X2

6 Detecting fraud

Internal controls within the accounting system should be designed not only to address weaknesses and prevent fraud and errors, but also to help detect when they have occurred.

The key controls that detect whether fraud or errors have occurred are:

(a) **Spot checks** on whether control activities have taken place

(b) **Performance reviews** and comparisons, using:

   (i) The **budgetary control report**: compare actual results to budgeted results

   (ii) **Ratio analysis**: compare this period to the previous period, and evaluate the relationships between figures in the financial statements (eg level of receivables compared with level of sales)

(c) **Reconciliation** of information produced by the accounting system with external evidence, such as bank statements and supplier statements

(d) **Control account reconciliations** where transactions are recorded in individual accounts and in total (eg receivables and payables)

7 Using financial information

Management can use financial information to analyse and review the controls of an organisation. Financial information can highlight issues such as potential inefficiencies as well as possible fraudulent behaviour, eg decreases in profit margin may suggest that costs are being poorly managed, or may highlight an issue such as theft of inventory.

7.1 Management accounts

Management reports can be structured to ensure that the most useful information is available to the user of the report. The information may be summarised into a form of income and expense statement, or include additional information such as variance analysis, aged receivables analysis or capital expenditure review for the period.

Ideally these reports should be consistently prepared, and monitored, on a regular basis, eg monthly, so as to highlight any significant issues arising, and to prompt investigations and corrective action where required.

Activity 5: Detecting fraud using financial information

Here are some extracts from the management accounts which were completed at the year end for CCC.

Use these and the financial statements in the pre-seen scenario for this activity.

CCC completes quarterly management accounts only.

Extracts from the management accounts for CCC Ltd as at 31 December 20X2

	20X2 Carpets £000	20X2 Vinyl £000	20X1 Carpets £000	20X1 Vinyl £000
Revenue	379	727	425	505
Cost of sales	(287)	(416)	(282)	(351)
Gross margin	**92**	**311**	**143**	**154**
	All products £000	£000	**All products** £000	£000
Rent and rates	30		30	
Salaries: administration and management	87		87	
Salaries: sales	105		60	
Salaries: directors	120		110	
Motor expenses	19		10	
Irrecoverable debts	22		8	
Other costs	18		16	
Total costs		**401**		**321**
Net profit/(loss)		**2**		**(24)**

Required

Using the knowledge you have obtained from the earlier chapters, review the management accounts above and highlight areas which present potential issues for the company, making any recommendations you believe are appropriate.

Note. There is no requirement to calculate ratios.

7.2 Budgetary control reports

A key report issued by the management accounting function, and assessable in the *Accounting Systems and Controls* unit, is the **budgetary control report**, or variance analysis report.

A **budgetary control report** compares standard costs and revenues with actual results, to obtain variances which highlight any deviations that managers should investigate to improve performance.

Activity 6: CCC budget control report

Below is the budgetary control report for March 20X3. CCC only prepares this once a quarter due to the level of work required and the ability of the staff to complete this in addition to their current workloads. Stefan, who has some AAT training, is responsible for completing this analysis. Stefan does not fully understand how fixed costs are absorbed, so he has left those bits blank for now. Stefan has included the cost of delivery and motor expenses in the variable cost calculation.

This analysis covers only the best-selling products, and is passed to the directors for their review. However, Stefan is unsure as to which areas are of most interest to the directors.

Here is a budgetary control report for the newly launched Wood Effect (Oak) in the Umteeko range for quarter 1 of 20X3.

CCC Ltd

Budgetary control report for the three months to March 20X3

	£	£	£	
Budgeted profit			21,000	
Sales volume profit variance			1,750	(Fav)
Standard profit from actual sales			22,750	

	£ Favourable	£ Adverse	£	
Variances				
Sales price	975			
Material price	200			
Material usage		7,500		
Labour rate	600			
Labour efficiency		4,250		
Variable overhead rate	125			
Variable overhead efficiency	350			
Fixed overhead expenditure	–			
Fixed overhead volume efficiency	–			
Fixed overhead volume capacity	–			
	2,250	11,750	9,500	(Adverse)
Actual profit			13,250	

Required

(a) Identify areas on which the directors should focus in more detail in the above budgetary control report.

(b) Comment on any limitations on the above budgetary information supplied.

The mechanics of how the standard costs are determined, and how the associated variances are calculated, are covered in the *Management Accounting: Budgeting* and *Management Accounting: Decision and Control* units, so are not covered here. The management accounting units also cover the meaning of these variances, and how they complement each other.

Understanding and communicating these aspects of the budgetary report are vital roles of the accounting function.

7.3 Ratio analysis

A key way in which statutory financial statements are analysed by both internal and external stakeholders is the application of **ratio analysis**.

Ratio analysis is making comparisons between figures in a company's financial statements and how they relate to each other in order to determine the financial performance and position of the company.

The mechanics of how ratios are calculated are covered in the Level 4 *Financial Statements of Limited Companies* unit so are not covered in detail here.

7.4 Scorecards

It is increasingly common for management accounting functions to produce **scorecards** incorporating both financial and non-financial ratios, and other indicators.

A scorecard should provide managers with information which addresses all relevant areas of performance, and in an objective and unbiased fashion.

Scorecards differ from ratio analysis in that they include non-financial information too.

Scorecards typically contain measures from at least four different perspectives, commonly including:

(a) **Customer satisfaction** – on issues that matter to customers: cost, quality, delivery, inspection, handling and so on

(b) **Process efficiency** – with the aim of improving internal processes, decision making and resource utilisation

(c) **Growth** – or the business's capacity to maintain its competitive position through the acquisition of new skills (training) and the development of new products (innovation)

(d) **Financial success** – including traditional measures, such as growth, profitability and shareholder value, with a clear focus on how value is created for all major stakeholders

The scorecard can be used to identify suitable targets for each measure, commensurate with the company's overall strategy. These targets can be cascaded to departmental managers, who are responsible for achieving them. In doing so goal congruence is embedded within the control system.

The advantages of the scorecard approach:

- It looks at both internal and external matters concerning the company.

- It is related to the key elements of a company's strategy.

- Financial and non-financial measures are linked together.

- There is a recognition that financial success is driven by non-financial factors, such as innovation, customer satisfaction and internal efficiency.

Key term

A **scorecard** is a performance management tool which addresses all relevant areas of performance, both financial and non-financial, in an objective and unbiased fashion.

Assessment focus point

Ensure that you can calculate the key ratios and can explain the results in relation to the scenario. Choose the ratios which are relevant to the question and the scenario. You may need to explain limitations of using such ratios as well.

Activity 7: Balanced scorecard and ratios

Below is a balanced scorecard drawn up by John Cookridge for CCC.

He has drawn up some of the objectives and how these can be measured.

| Financial success | | Customer satisfaction | |
Objectives	Measures	Objectives	Measures
To be profitable	Financial results	Great service	Repeat business
		Excellent range of quality products	New products that sell to the local customer base

| Process efficiency | | Growth | |
Objectives	Measures	Objectives	Measures
Efficient staff	Staff meeting realistic targets for fitting and delivery times	Trained staff	Employees with relevant training and qualifications
Ethical treatment of suppliers	Pay suppliers on time	Becoming the largest independent flooring provider in the region	Increase in market share

Required

Using the information regarding the objectives and measures used by CCC in its balanced scorecard, together with financial information in the scenario, answer the following:

(a) **Comment on the profitability of the company, using appropriate ratios with explanations.**

(b) **Consider the customer satisfaction objectives and measures used by CCC, and make recommendations on how the company can improve data and feedback on them to management.**

(c) **CCC bases its process efficiency measures on the efficiency of staff and paying suppliers on time. Using ratios where appropriate, analyse whether CCC are meeting these objectives.**

(d) **Using the stated objectives used by CCC regarding its growth metrics, make recommendations on how the company can improve on its reporting measures, ensuring management obtain accurate and useful information.**

8 Fraud matrix

A **fraud matrix** is a map of the potential frauds against an organisation, cross-referenced to the risks of each of these occurring, documenting the controls over these risks.

A fraud matrix helps the company:

- Investigate the **potential** for fraud within a system
- Analyse the **controls** currently in place to prevent fraud
- **Grade the potential** for fraud, according to risk

Although this approach is subjective, it enables a risk-based approach to improving controls that are appropriate to the company.

The risk to the company is graded on an appropriate scale, either numerically on a scale of 1–5 or by stating the deemed level of risk:

- 1 = low
- 3 = medium
- 5 = high

Possible improvements to the controls for all high and/or medium risks can then be recommended.

8.1 Identifying the grade of risk

The level of risk of fraud in a particular situation is graded as high, medium or low by identifying two factors:

- The **likelihood** of the risk occurring; and
- The potential **impact** of that risk on the company.

Illustration 1

In looking at the potential for the misappropriation of petty cash in CCC:

- The likelihood is high (5): loose cash is easy to steal and it presents a strong temptation, especially in small amounts, as the person stealing it may not perceive the loss to be that 'bad' a thing for the company.

- The impact on the company is medium (3), as the company could potentially lose £1,200.

Combining these two factors, the overall risk of fraud in relation to petty cash would probably be graded as medium/high (4).

Activity 8: Fraud matrix CCC

Using your knowledge obtained to date of CCC answer the following questions. Use the table given to guide your answer.

Required

Complete the fraud matrix below in respect of CCC. In particular you should:

(a) Identify FOUR risks to CCC which may not be prevented or detected by the existing controls currently in place

(b) Identify any regulation or law which could be broken by CCC as a result of these risks and the possible impact on the organisation

Potential fraud	Controls currently in place	Risk to CCC 1 = low, 5 = high	Implications/ Regulations affected
1			
2			
3			
4			

Chapter summary

- Fraud is a crime in which the company suffers a loss because someone either misappropriates assets or misstates information in the financial statements.

- Misappropriation can take the form of: theft of assets; teeming and lading of receipts (sales ledger) and payments (purchases ledger); setting up fictitious suppliers, employees or customers; collusion with customers and suppliers; paying for goods and services not received by the company; and disposal of assets without authority.

- Misstatement of the financial statements arises from: over- or undervaluing inventory; not writing off irrecoverable debts; manipulating accounting estimates to affect profit; fictitious sales; and understating expenses.

- Prevention controls for fraud comprise: authorisation; segregation of duties; reconciliation procedures; and review procedures.

- Fraud controls for the accounting system are categorised as staff, management, physical and computer controls.

- A fraud matrix maps potential frauds to the risk to the company and controls over that risk.

- The risk of fraud is graded from low (1) to high (5) on the fraud matrix; more attention is devoted to internal controls over the higher risks.

- Detection controls over fraud comprise: spot checks; performance reviews; reconciliation procedures; and control accounts.

- Ratio analysis is a key way in which statutory financial statements are analysed by both internal and external stakeholders.

- Sales system frauds are typically: stealing cash receipts; overcharging for sales; inflating customer orders; writing off debts; raising credit notes; and teeming and lading.

- Purchases system frauds include: ordering goods for own use; paying fictitious suppliers; paying funds into personal bank accounts; and teeming and lading.

- Payroll system frauds may involve: ghost employees; overstating overtime pay; unauthorised increases in pay rates; false expense reimbursements; and retained leavers.

- Fraud affects the company in terms of: financial loss; reputational damage; and poor employee morale.

- A fraud matrix can allow an organisation to consider the potential frauds and grade the risks, allowing management to focus on the areas of priority first.

- The balanced scorecard is a performance management tool which addresses all relevant areas of performance, both financial and non-financial, in an objective and unbiased fashion.

Keywords

- **Budgetary control report:** This compares standard costs and revenues with actual results, to obtain variances which highlight any deviations that managers should investigate to improve performance

- **Fraud controls:** Internal controls specifically against fraud in the areas of staff controls, management controls, physical controls and IT controls

- **Fraud matrix:** A map of the potential frauds against an organisation, cross-referenced to the risks of each of these occurring, documenting the controls over these risks

- **Misappropriation of assets:** Theft, teeming and lading, payment of false employees or suppliers

- **Misstatement of financial statements:** Overstating assets or profit, or understating profit, losses or liabilities

- **Ratio analysis:** Making comparisons between figures in a company's financial statements and how they relate to each other in order to determine the financial performance and position of the company

- **Risk of fraud:** The likelihood of the fraud occurring and its impact if it does occur

Test your learning

1 **Which of the following is a type of fraud covered by the Fraud Act 2006?**

	✓
False accounting	
False representation	
Misstatement of the financial statements	
Misappropriation of assets	

2 **Complete the following statement:**

Internal audit activities are a type of _____ over fraud in the accounting system.

Picklist:

application control
management control
physical control
staff control

3 **Which TWO factors are evaluated to grade the risk of fraud in a fraud matrix?**

	✓
Time	
Responsibility	
Likelihood	
Volatility	
Impact	

4 **The THREE categories of impact of fraud on a company are:**

	✓
Morale	
Social	
Reputation	
Environmental	
Financial	

5 **Which of the following statements is correct?**

	✓
During the analysis of the sales system, a fraud matrix graded the potential loss from misappropriation to be rated 5. Management have decided urgent action is required.	
A fraud matrix is a subjective analysis of an organisation's controls, and will ensure that all recommendations identified are actioned immediately.	
A control within the payroll system has been rated as 2 within the fraud matrix. Management have decided that this risk must be rectified immediately.	

Making changes to systems

6

Learning outcomes

1.3	**Examine the impact of relevant regulations affecting the accounting function**
	• Assess how the existing structure of the accounting function may need to be adapted to comply with changes in external regulations
1.4	**Demonstrate an understanding of the impact of management information requirements on the accounting function**
	• Why changes may be required to existing systems to meet revised organisation requirements
3.4	**Examine current and planned methods of operating**
	• Explain that appropriate controls need to be in place during the transition from one system to another
4.1	**Identify changes to the accounting system or parts of the accounting system**
	• Identify suitable changes to the accounting system
	• Explain any assumptions made
	• Identify problems that might occur during transition
4.2	**Analyse the implications of changes to the accounting system**
	• Quantify the costs of recommendations, stating assumptions made
	• Undertake a cost-benefit analysis
	• Evaluate the implications of the changes to operating procedures and time spent
4.3	**Consider the effects of recommended changes on users of the system**
	• Identify the changes that users may be required to make to working practices to comply with changes to statutory and organisational requirements
	• Consider different methods of support that can be given to users of the accounting system to assist them in adapting to the recommended changes
4.4	**Justify recommended changes to the accounting system**
	• Effectively present recommendations to management
	• Provide a clear rationale to support recommendations

Assessment context

Assessment of these topics will be included within a number of tasks in the synoptic assessment at Level 4.

Qualification context

While this chapter draws on costing principles covered at Levels 2 and 3, for the most part its content is new.

Business context

Management should regularly review the accounting systems for relevance and to ensure that it is working as originally intended. As businesses grow and change, so do the accounting systems within them, therefore management should be ensuring that regular review is undertaken.

Systemic weaknesses in accounting systems require changes to be made, otherwise the system may potentially be exposed to fraud and error. Any system changes need to be thoroughly evaluated to ensure they deliver a value for money solution.

Changes made to the accounting system must be carefully planned and controls put in place to ensure that the business can continue during the time of transition.

Chapter overview

* Tangible
  costs/benefits
* Intangible
  costs/benefits
* Opportunity cost
* Relevant costs
* Other factors
* Justification of the
  new system
* Implementation
  plan

Introduction

This chapter looks at what happens when organisations make changes to their accounting system and internal controls.

To ensure any planned changes generate benefits, the preparation of a **cost-benefit analysis** should be undertaken. This helps management identify and understand all of the relevant costs associated with implementing system changes, and the benefits that will be gained from doing so.

Costs and benefits may be **tangible**, meaning that they can be quantified, or **intangible**, meaning they are harder to assess, as they cannot be quantified in monetary terms.

Included in any analysis should be the **opportunity costs** of any actions eg if money is spent on a new system you should consider where else this could be spent within the organisation eg on sales promotions or new product development.

Aside from the financial aspects it will also be important to assess the impact that any proposed changes will have on staff and other stakeholders.

1 Identifying the need for change

In the previous chapters of this Course Book, we have identified situations where change may be needed in an accounting function, an accounting system or an internal control system. The need for change can sometimes become apparent when deploying many of the tools we have seen previously eg SWOT, fraud matrices, ratios, key performance indicators and scorecards.

1.1 Reasons for review

Management often have specific reasons to undertake detailed reviews of accounting systems:

Personnel changes	Changes in management or departments
	Department mergers or changes (such as launching a new range of products or diversification)
	Rapid hiring of staff to meet demand
	High turnover of staff
Company strategy change	Change in focus for the company strategy
	Acquisition of a new business (such as in a merger, or takeover) or sale of a business sector
Technology changes	New software or hardware
	Changes in cyber security (possibly as a result of a cyber attack or the threat of one)

Financial reasons	Management have identified areas requiring cost reduction
	Development of a new market for the product (such as overseas)
	Analysis of costs highlighting adverse ratios with similar companies in the same industry

1.2 Timely and regular review

Even if there are no specific reasons to prompt a review of the accounting systems, policies and controls, the systems should still be reviewed on a timely basis.

Often there may be small, incremental changes which are not sufficiently significant to generate a full review of the system, such as a replacement head of department (there is still a supervisor, and the systems are still working as before). However, over time, these small changes may cause an accounting system to be less effective, less efficient or no longer fit for purpose.

Changes occurring over time	The system may require additional stages in the process, eg additional authorising staff to cover more purchasing
	Changes in authorisation levels to reflect current spending
	Alteration of the holiday approval process to spread 'peak periods' more fairly across staff (no longer first come, first served)
	Monthly invoice payment runs changed to weekly
	Weekly paid staff to be paid monthly
	Moving from cash payments to staff to online banking for salaries and expenses
Post implementation review	Perhaps a new system has been installed but changes are required to improve it.
	The process of reviewing new systems once they are 'up and running' can elicit further changes

Efficiencies	Efficiencies may be identified which can reduce cost, waste or time: • Using online banking instead of cheques • E-receipts instead of paper • Online ordering process instead of telephone based
Identifying problems before they occur	The current system may be working, but it may be flawed. How does it work in practice compared to how it looks on paper. There may be steps required by overworked line managers which can be shared, automated or changed. If the current system is open to neglect or abuse, then problems may occur. A pre-emptive review of key areas may highlight areas for revision.

1.3 Changes in regulation or statutory requirements

Management need to ensure that they comply with all existing regulatory requirements; however, it is also essential that they keep abreast of any future regulatory changes which may affect their organisation.

Accounting standards change on a regular basis, and occasionally these changes will also affect the information that the organisation will be required to provide.

For instance, IFRS 15 *Revenue from Contracts with Customers* requires companies to provide additional information regarding the costing and contractual revenue on long-term contracts. In this example, the company will need to ensure that this additional information is constantly updated to avoid leaving itself with a huge task at year end. Management will need to ensure that their monthly reporting is robust enough to supply the information required at year end, and to avoid any 'shocks' when the financial results are published.

Other changes which have affected organisations in recent years include:

• Online RTI payroll reporting to HM Revenue & Customs regarding payroll payments and deductions made to staff

• Revised Money Laundering regulations, increasing the checks and measures that a company must perform on new staff

• Revised waste management disposal regulations and increased requirements regarding disposal and recycling

An organisation must therefore have an eye on future developments and ensure that changes are not left until the last minute.

Assessment focus point

Not all changes are dictated by operational or organisational need. New statutory or legal requirements may force working practices or accounting system changes onto an organisation. It is therefore essential for an organisation to be aware of potential changes to ensure they have sufficient time to implement them ahead of regulatory deadlines.

Activity 1: Business regulations

Use the information provided on CCC.

Required

(a) Consider the potential weaknesses in the organisation being able to keep up to date and have a 'long-term view' on potential changes which may affect it.

(b) Make any recommendations for improvement, relevant to the scenario.

2 Types of change

The type of change required can be assessed by analysing:

(a) The **seriousness of the problem** to be resolved – changing a system riddled with inherent weaknesses or subject to fraud is evidently a much bigger job than ensuring an upgrade of an existing off-the-shelf payroll package.

(b) The **scope of the change** – implementing a completely new accounting system is more of a challenge than revising the responsibilities of two members of staff.

(c) The **context** in which change takes place – changes needed to safeguard jobs may be easier to implement than those that staff perceive to be cosmetic in nature, or unnecessary.

The degree of change can be classified as the following:

• **Transformational change** is a wholesale change, eg integrating all accounting functions at a centralised location with a new computer system.

• **Incremental change** is a small change or a big change made in small steps eg gradually moving each sub-system on to an integrated accounting package.

The type of change will depend on what the issues are and how management decide to proceed with the changes. This is covered later in the chapter.

3 Cost-benefit analysis

A cost-benefit analysis takes recommendations for changes and improvements in the accounting system and its controls and analyses them in terms of the costs and benefits to the company of implementing them.

Change should be cost effective in that the benefits of the change should outweigh its costs.

Both costs and benefits can be tangible and intangible.

Key term

> **Cost-benefit analysis** analyses recommendations for change in terms of the costs and benefits to the company of implementing them.

A simple **cost-benefit analysis** may look something like this:

	£'000	£'000
Initial costs		
Cost of machinery	500	
Staff training	75	
Site preparation	10	
		585
Annual running costs		
Safety checks (req'd every 2100 hours of production)	150	
Replacement drill heads	14	
		164
Total costs over lifetime (5 years)		749
Savings		
Staff hours savings	25	
Costs of running the old machinery (5 × 155)	775	
		800
Total net benefit over 5 years		**51**

In order to produce an accurate and meaningful cost-benefit analysis, it is necessary to ensure all costs and benefits are included.

3.1 Tangible costs

Tangible costs are relatively easy to value as they can be quantified in terms of time and/or money.

> **Illustration 1**
>
> The tangible costs of a recommended new computer system are the quantifiable cost of:
>
> - The system itself (training, hardware and software)
> - The loss of staff time while they are training
> - Software licences
> - Future upgrades to maintain speed of processing or due to technical updates regarding regulation or other changes

Tangible costs are identified, quantifiable costs of the change eg buying a new software package.

Activity 2: Tangible cost of a new system

CCC has decided to investigate using an accountancy software package called KashCade.

There are three part-time staff in the accounting department, and they are considering adding a full-time member. The directors cannot decide how they will ensure staff are adequately trained. They are also considering whether the warehouse team and the sales team will require system access too. The estimated cost of the sales team being away for a day is expected to be £2,000 in lost sales, with the total cost of using temporary staff in the accounts team whilst they undergo training of £540 (per day).

CCC have used an external consultant (at a cost of £750) who has estimated that the increase in efficiencies will save CCC £6,300 per year. This is in addition to the expected increase in sales (of £5,000 for the first year, increasing by 15% each year) due to the ability to make online sales and reduce inventory holding and tying up cash.

KashCade has broken down the elements of the system as follows:

> Dear Sirs
>
> Thank you for your interest in our integrated accounting system. We are happy to provide you with details of the following:
>
> - Basic System 1 (Cloud).
> - Sales ledger system, including pre-numbered invoices and aged debt reports
> - Purchases ledger system, incorporating purchase orders which can be matched against incoming invoices. Inventory aging reports are included.
> - General ledger and summary trial balance reports.
> - Journal functionality.
> - Exception reporting.
> - Budget input and comparison tools.
> - Updates and upgrades occur regularly and will be automated at no extra cost.
>
> Additional add-ons which can be purchased:
>
> - Payroll function which will also integrate with the general ledger and allow full Real Time Information (RTI) to HM Revenue & Customs, as well as year-end reporting and payslip production.
> - Draft financial statements reporting.

- Advanced inventory option which allocates a FIFO cost and monitors the current inventory cost, allocating costs to allow a 'cost of project' for each customer.

Annual costs

	Initial costs	Annual costs
Basic system 1 (cloud)	£5,000 (to cover assistance with data migration)	£3,250 (up to 10 licensed users)
Payroll	–	£550
Financial accounts	–	£750
Advanced inventory	–	£1,250

We also recommend using our training partner, Best Practical Performance Ltd, to supply the training to staff on the KashCade system.

In-house training (maximum of 15 people) 2 days	£3,500
Course at local college (3 days)	£350 per person
Online course (completed in own time)	£75 per person (licence limited to access for 6 months)

We can include a full support system, 24 hours a day by remote operators for £250 per year, with the first year free of charge.

If you have any further questions, please do not hesitate to contact us.

Yours sincerely

P. Bryan

Sales Director
KashCade Ltd

Required

Prepare a report showing a brief financial cost-benefit analysis, together with additional narrative. Ensure that the following have been included in your report:

(a) **Identify the tangible costs of this purchasing decision.**

(b) **Estimate the overall costs of purchasing this software. Consider also how CCC could reduce these costs, and the implications of doing so. Assume that the software will initially be used for 5 years.**

Where the information regarding the actual cost cannot be defined (due to insufficient available information), show how it may be an issue in the narrative to your report.

(Hint: Think of costs not just in terms of money spent but also in relation to time and any other quantifiable measure.)

3.5 Benefits

There should be at least some tangible and/or intangible benefits of any changes made to the accounting system, otherwise there is no point making them.

Tangible benefits may be more difficult to quantify than tangible costs, but easy to identify eg less time spent creating invoices, improved efficiency.

Intangible benefits are benefits of the change that are more difficult to identify and quantify eg improved reputation for efficiency, improving the customer experience in a showroom, facilitating an increase in the amount of time spent browsing, or making conditions for staff better so that they are more motivated at work.

It may not be possible to put estimated values against every benefit, especially intangible ones, but describing the benefits clearly is extremely important in a cost-benefit analysis. These often form powerful arguments in favour of implementing a recommendation.

A systems change may be due to the availability of a new software package, improving the information which is available to management from the raw data input by the employees. This can increase staff morale, as they are able to work more efficiently or may benefit from the automation of mundane manual tasks. A new system may offer new opportunities for retention of customers or attracting new customers, such as loyalty programmes or bonuses for referring friends to the company.

Activity 4: Benefits of training

Consider again the training discussed in Activities 2 and 3.

Required

What intangible benefits might there be in sending CCC's staff on the training programme?

3.6 Other factors to consider

Aside from the costs and benefits already discussed in this chapter, there are other considerations which will impact how an organisation approaches a potential change, or assesses whether it is necessary to change or not.

Using a SWOT analysis (as discussed in Chapter 4) or the scorecard approach (in Chapter 5) can help to focus management's attention on the areas that need

The aim is to give a best view of the main issues and where the costs are to be spent.

The plan should not only cover financial costs, but also consider the morale of staff, including when to inform them of the changes, how often to update them and how this can be best be carried out.

Activity 5: Cost-benefit analysis

Use the information you have been provided with to date, including the answers to the activities in this chapter.

Required

Prepare a detailed cost-benefit report for the two directors which provides an analysis for implementing a centralised, integrated accounting system in CCC, with appropriate staff training.

Note. Where you cannot quantify either costs or benefits, you should indicate with '£X' within the analysis where a quantified cost or benefit could be determined.

4 Making the change

There are various factors which should be reflected on by management when considering the process for change within an organisation.

4.1 Change process

The main elements of the change process can be described in the following flow chart.

Evaluate
- Evaluate the system and its problems – determine that the particular change required is actually necessary eg is there a regulatory change that requires a system update? Systems should be evaluated prior to proposing any recommendations.
- If a system is working sufficiently well, it may mean that the recommended change is not required.

Recommend
- Proposal of a solution to the identified problem
- Consider any previous attempts to correct problems and mitigate for possible issues (busy seasons, such as year end, Christmas, holiday periods, availability of key personnel)
- Expertise: Are experts or contractors required to assist with the implementation (or even additional staff to help out with day to day roles when key staff are involved in the implementation?)

Communication
- Clear communication of the proposed changes to all relevant stakeholders, including users of the new systems and those who receive information (such as monthly reports) from it
- Give a rationale behind the change and the reasons for it
- Explain when and how the changes will take place
- Consider any feedback and whether plans may need to be adjusted accordingly
- Agreed change initially takes longer, as everyone has to 'buy in' to it, but it can be faster overall than forced change as residual resistance is generally lower once the new system is implemented.

Training
- Staff will need to be trained on the new system, this may be new software or adapting to the new policies and procedures to be put in place
- Consider how will staff be trained to ensure they are familiar with the new system, but minimise disruption to the main business of the organisation

Implementation
- Draw up a timetable for change
- Consider using running systems side for side for a period to ensure no disruption to the business
- Consider whether all precautions been taken to ensure there are no 'gaps' which may be opportunities for system failure, potential fraud or loss of information

Review
- Review the effectiveness of the change – has the problem identified been remedied as intended? You may need to make further changes if not.

4.2 Resistance to change

Individuals working within a system tend to put up barriers to change (eg objecting, staging a 'go slow', disputing every detail), even when the change is perfectly valid and even when it is quite small. This is because most people fear change, or rather they fear the uncertainty that surrounds change.

Managers need to be aware of these concerns, and think about how best to overcome the inevitable resistance they will face when planning system changes.

With any proposed and significant change, it is advisable to communicate the reasons and discuss with staff why the change is happening, eg discussions with trade unions, staff representatives, regular updates (email or face to face).

Activity 6: Issues during transition

The directors of CCC have decided to investigate how to improve the computer and reporting systems of the accounts team. They are considering the following proposals:

(a)   The introduction of an integrated accounting system which will require new training for everyone who uses it, including warehouse staff and sales staff.

(b)   Strict reporting deadlines regarding aged receivables reporting and high-level monthly management accounts.

(c)   Recruiting a full-time senior qualified accountant to oversee the accounting function.

Required

Identify any problems which may arise at CCC when implementing any of the above proposals.

5 Transition process

Any implementation of a new system or changes to the existing processes should be carefully controlled, including monitoring to ensure there is minimal disruption to normal daily business whilst maintaining sufficient controls to prevent errors or potential fraud.

There need to be strong controls over the implementation of the new system and the transition across from the old one.

5.1 Transformational change

As we saw earlier, this is a wholesale change from one system to another on a designated date. Effectively, 'flicking the switch' from one system to another. Without detailed and careful planning, this can result in disarray, however, for smaller, less complex businesses moving from simple systems (such as paper based or simple spreadsheet) this is often the most cost effective method

5.2 Phased change

For some organisations, switching from one system to another in one go is too risky or their systems are too complex to complete in an orderly fashion. Phased change has a series of milestones, with key dates where changes are made. For example, the new system may be launched on smaller parts of the business first, such as HR or non-current assets, before moving onto more integrated systems such as purchases and inventory management. Although the process takes longer than the transformational change, it allows a review of the process at each stage, making changes where required to ensure the next process runs more smoothly.

5.3 Parallel systems

This is where the old and the new system run in parallel with each other, effectively doubling the workload, eg the staff have to enter the sales orders into two systems instead of one. This does allow an element of 'live testing' so ensuring that the new system can cope with the organisation's requirements, however, it is generally a more costly approach, albeit one which is less risky in terms of lost data, or errors in the system.

5.4 Controls over the move to the new system

New systems are often tested prior to using live data, so running a set of test data to ensure that it will provide the reports and the analysis required for the organisation. Sometimes, the system will be 'piloted' in one area of the business only, this allows management to understand the main benefits and downsides of switching to the new system. Often, only a small group of staff are used to run this piloted system before management decide to proceed with a larger implementation organisation-wide.

Management need to ensure strong controls over the movement of existing data across to the new system. This is discussed at the planning stage to ensure that any consultants are aware of the extent of the data, and the level of required access to it by staff (such as to provide information to prepare financial statements or to support a tax audit). This 'migration of data' to the new system will be carefully managed, and require testing to ensure none is lost in the transition.

Illustration

If the management of CCC decide to implement a new accounting system, there needs to be a series of controls regarding the practical aspect of moving the organisation onto the new system.

Management will need to be able to answer a number of questions:

(a) **Existing system** – what will happen to the existing system? Will it be switched off or archived? Maybe it will run 'in parallel' with the new system for a set period of time (this may be tricky as twice the amount of work may have to be undertaken, but it allows for a level of guarantee and security should the new system suffer teething problems).

(b) **Existing data** – how will the existing data be transferred onto the new system? Will it be manually entered or taken across in a 'migration'? How reliable is the old data; will it need cleansing before it is migrated onto the new system?

(c) **Training of staff** – some staff may need to be used in the implementation of the project, so considering who will be trained and when this will happen is important. There may be a need to use temporary staff or external consultants.

(d) **Leadership** – all changes should be monitored, perhaps using a project tool to ensure that milestones are achieved on time, and other issues dealt with as soon as possible.

(e) **Timing** – ensuring that the change is planned in detail, and arranged for a time which best suits CCC.

(f) **Security** – how can you ensure that the old system is no longer accessible (either deliberately or inadvertently) by staff? Consider the level of access required for each member of staff on the new system; this may be an opportunity to implement stricter controls and segregation.

Activity 7: Implementation of a new system

Use the information on CCC which you have analysed to date, including the information in earlier chapters.

Required

(a) **Consider THREE potential risks and concerns specific to CCC which may cause issues with the implementation of the new system.**

(b) **Propose any remedial actions which management should consider.**

Risks and concerns regarding the new system at CCC	Potential remedial actions

Chapter summary

- Change may be needed to an accounting system because it contains systemic weaknesses that make it prone to fraud and error.

- The degree of change necessary depends on: the seriousness of the problem; the scope of the change; and the context in which the change will take place.

- A cost-benefit analysis will enable management to assess the level of change required and whether an alternative option may be preferred.

- To numerically analyse the decision to proceed with a decision (shutdown, make or buy decisions), the relevant costs of a project should be evaluated.

- Costs and benefits may be tangible, such as improved efficiencies, improved customer service or decreased operational costs. These tangible costs can be measured.

- The intangible costs and benefits are harder to quantify, such as improved employee morale due to a better working environment.

- A change may be transformational or incremental.

- The prospect of change can meet with resistance from employees, management, shareholders or customers. It is vital that the expectations and fears of these stakeholders are considered and mitigated in advance of any change occurring.

- Steps for making a change to the accounting system: analyse the system and its problems; choose how to make the change; prepare a plan for making the change; analyse the likely reactions of stakeholders; draw up a timetable for change; communicate the plan and its timetable; make the change; and monitor the effectiveness of the change.

- The transition from one system to another should be planned and controlled to ensure no loss of data and to minimise disruption to the organisation, its employees and customers.

- System changes may be required due to regulatory or legislative changes.

Keywords

- **Incremental change:** A small change or a big change made in small steps eg gradually moving each sub-system onto an integrated accounting package

- **Intangible benefits:** Benefits of the change that are more difficult to identify and quantify eg improved reputation for efficiency

- **Intangible costs:** Costs of the change that are more difficult to identify and quantify eg the cost of lost custom as customers go elsewhere during the disruption caused by the change

- **Tangible benefits:** May be more difficult to quantify than tangible costs, but easy to identify eg less time spent creating invoices, improved efficiency

- **Tangible costs:** Identified, quantifiable costs of the change eg buying a new software package

- **Transformational change:** A wholesale change, eg integrating all accounting functions at a centralised location with a new computer system

Test your learning

1   Ard Ltd is a large business with many operating centres. To date its accounting has been done using various software packages on an independent PC at each operating centre. Ard Ltd now plans to move to a centralised accounting function with an integrated accounting system.

    Complete the following statement.

    Ard Ltd's plan is _____ change.

    Picklist:

    an incremental
    a transformational

2   **Complete the following statement.**

    The fact that Ard Ltd's staff in its operating centres will no longer use the skills they have developed in accounting is

	✓
a tangible cost of the change.	
an intangible benefit of the change.	
a tangible benefit of the change.	
an intangible cost of the change.	

3   **Complete the following statement.**

    The fact that Ard Ltd's employees will be disrupted by the planned change, so will not be able to work on an alternative new project, is an _____ of the change.

    Picklist:

    inevitable consequence
    intangible benefit
    opportunity cost

4   In the process of integrating its accounting system Ard Ltd has discovered some misappropriation of assets and has dismissed the accountant responsible.

    Complete the following statement.

    This is an example of _____ change, and ensuring the system is effective following such a change is likely to take _____.

    Picklist:

    a forced
    an agreed
    little time
    some time

5 **Complete the following statement.**

Change should be _____ in that the benefits of the change should outweigh its costs.

Picklist:

cost effective
cost neutral
cost efficient

6 There are several situations which may cause an organisation to review their controls and accounting systems.

Using the picklist provided, select the correct answer for each of the following situations

	Reason
A merger of the treasury and the finance function	▼
Management accounts report that the costs for the warehouse department are consistently running above budget	▼
The sales team to be issued with tablet computers to allow them to place orders and check inventory levels, whilst with customers in the showroom	▼
The directors are discontinuing one of the less profitable products, resulting in a refocus on the remaining three core products instead	▼

Picklist:

Company strategy change
Financial change
Personnel change
Technological change

CHAPTER 1 Introduction to the organisation

Activity 1: Internal stakeholders

(a) Directors of CCC

- Management accounts to review the overall performance of the company.

- Aged receivables and payables reports to ensure that payments are being made on time to suppliers and that customers' cash is being collected on a timely basis. This is necessary for cash flow management.

- Margin analysis on the products or types of products being sold, to verify whether lines should be continued or replaced. Given that the market for carpet is being squeezed, and CCC has the local market in the Umteeko range, consider whether the organisation should focus on that longer term.

If this information is not received, there is a risk that the company will not be able to react quickly enough to changes in the market. Cash flow control is vital in a small organisation; if peaks and troughs in cash flow are not correctly managed, the organisation may have to resort to expensive emergency overdrafts or may be unable to take advantage of any bulk order or early settlement discounts which suppliers may offer.

By reviewing the margins and relative profitability of the different types of product, CCC can react more quickly to the market conditions and ensure that they have enough inventory in their more popular lines. Currently, only two members of the fitting team are Umteeko trained which, given the popularity of the product and CCC's regional monopoly on the distribution, seems on the low side. CCC may be at risk of missing an opportunity to develop this line of business to replace its reduced turnover from more traditional floorings, such as carpets and tiles.

(b) Warehouse manager

- Inventory levels – what items are in stock and what has not moved for a long time (this inventory may need to be provided against or written off)

- Sales forecast – what inventory needs to be purchased to ensure that customers receive their products in a timely manner

- Supplier delivery and purchases schedule to ensure that inventory deliveries are as expected and can be verified to what has been ordered, and that there is sufficient room in the warehouse

- Liaison with the operations manager to ensure that the inventory will be available when the fitters are booked in to fit the product

Without strict inventory controls, stock may not be in when the fitters are booked in to deliver and fit the products. This will be a waste of resource (fitter time) and risks upsetting the customer who was expecting their carpet or flooring to be fitted on a set date.

(c) Operations manager

- Sales order information to plan the fitters and delivery routes for the week/month ahead

- Vacation details from payroll (to avoid everyone going on holiday at the same time, especially staff with specific skills or training)

- Liaison with the warehouse manager to ensure that the inventory will be available when the fitters are booked in to fit the product, otherwise this may cause problems with customer relations in terms of expectation of delivery

(d) Payroll clerk

- Details of new starters/leavers.

- Information on pay rises authorised by management.

- Overtime information authorised by the operations manager, to ensure that overtime is correctly paid on time.

- Sales commission information authorised by the sales manager, to ensure that all commission has been verified by the sales manager and paid in a timely manner.

- Vacation and sickness details authorised by line managers, to ensure that vacation pay is correctly allocated and details of sickness (and any sick pay) are logged and monitored.

- Contracts for all staff (to ensure pay is set at the correct level).

- Cash flow information to ensure that there is sufficient money to pay the staff. If staff cannot be paid on time, there is a risk of employee discontent and losing skilled members of the workforce.

Activity 2: External stakeholders

Key external stakeholders for CCC are likely to include some or all of the following:

- Customers, to ensure that the company is solvent eg if they have paid their deposit they have some security in CCC being able to supply their product.

- Suppliers, especially any significant or new suppliers who will be assessing CCC for creditworthiness. It will be helpful for CCC's cash flow to be able to buy supplies on credit.

- The Government, including HM Revenue & Customs (for PAYE and corporation tax) and the Registrar of Companies to ensure that the financial statements are filed on time.

- Lenders, such as the bank. Because CCC has an overdraft and a loan the lender will monitor CCC's solvency to ensure it is able to pay off its debts.

- Competitors can access information about CCC as they can view the statutory financial statements from the Registrar of Companies. Although for a small company like CCC the information may be limited to a statement of financial position, and small companies like CCC would want to minimise the amount of information a competitor would be able to view, provided they adhere to financial reporting regulations.

- Regulatory bodies would also be interested in the performance of the organisation, and if a complaint is made against the company there may be further inquiry by consumer groups.

- Umteeko would also have an interest in the performance of CCC. They will be keen to ensure that only trained fitters and approved adhesives are being used with its product. They would also want to view the company's overall performance, as Umteeko relies upon CCC for the sales of their product in the area. There is always a risk for CCC that poor performance on their part could mean that Umteeko decide to use another company to act as their local distributor.

Activity 3: Financial statements

As CCC is a small company, the external reporting information available publicly may be restricted to the statement of financial position and the notes and accounting policies. Nevertheless, this will be of use to the customers, suppliers and lenders as they will be able to verify the solvency of the company. However, this will only be at a certain point in the financial year (31 December) and will not give an up to date picture of the financial health of a company.

The bank may require further details, such as management accounts and cash flow statements, to verify that CCC can continue to pay its debts. This information would normally only be available to internal stakeholders. Additionally, there may be specific loan covenants – such as a stated level of interest cover that must be contractually supplied to the lender.

HM Revenue & Customs will want a detailed set of financial statements (companies must now provide detailed financial statements that are not abridged for tax purposes). Again, this information is only produced once a year and is not a guarantee that the tax will be paid on time or whether the company will default on its payments.

HM Revenue & Customs also requires monthly information on the payroll (Real Time Information reporting), which will ensure that payroll deductions are made correctly each month and the monies paid across in a timely manner.

Activity 4: Cash flows

The statement of cash flows separates out the net cash flows during the reporting period arising from:

- Operating activities (net profit for the period plus changes in current assets and liabilities excluding non-cash items). Depreciation is added back as this is not a cash flow from the business so cash in from trading was actually £9,000.

- Movements in working capital as represented by the increase or decrease in the balances for receivables, payables and inventories. In this period there was a net outflow of £21,000 represented by:

    - Inventory increasing by £24,000, so CCC is holding more stock

    - Receivables increasing by £51,000 as a result of higher sales in the year

    - Payables increasing by £47,000 as a result of increased purchases to support higher sales and inventory levels

- Investing activities (buying or disposing of non-current assets) so £2,000 was spent on new assets for use in the business and existing ones sold but bringing £5,000 into the business.

- Financing activities (paying dividends, taking out or paying back loans, issuing new shares). The financing costs of the loan and the overdraft came to £5,000 for last year, partially offsetting the £60,000 received from the new loan taken out.

- All of the above cash flows are then reconciled to the opening and closing cash positions – the balance of the cash at hand less the overdraft. Overall this has increased by £39,000, largely as a result of the £60,000 loan taken out in the year.

- The statement therefore summarises where the business has generated its cash in the year, and what it has spent its cash on in the period.

Activity 5: Ethical and sustainability information

Stakeholder	Information likely to be interested in
Customers	• Mission statement stating CCC's intention to behave ethically towards its customers. • Recycling information in the directors' report in the financial statement and the mission statement highlighting its 'green' credentials, which is important to any customers who are seeking more sustainable suppliers. • Looking to open new stores across the South coast, stating that the future is promising, and the company is looking ahead to expand further in the region.
Suppliers	• Mission statement stating CCC's intention to behave ethically towards its suppliers. • Information regarding CCC's potential move away from carpets and towards vinyl (implicit in the directors' report) may signal to carpet suppliers to offer bigger discounts to CCC or attract other vinyl suppliers to approach CCC.
Employees	• Mission statement stating that it supports diverse needs and behaves ethically towards its staff may attract new employees with physical or other disabilities to consider CCC when applying for employment. • Information in the directors' report stating that the company is a going concern and expansion may offer additional opportunities to staff keen to develop their skills and experience within CCC.
Ethical information	
Investors	• Some investors may want more information regarding the specific ethical actions of the business. For example, some will invest in companies which recycle or have strong 'green' credentials. The mission statement and directors' report both make statements to this effect at CCC. • Information in the directors' report concerning the expansion of stores, the contract with Umteeko and its aims to reduce costs that the company should be likely to continue for the foreseeable future. The information also demonstrates that management are aware of the limitations of the current market conditions and what they are doing to mitigate these risks.

Activity 6: Regulations

Scenario	What regulations should be adhered to	Expected controls required to be in place
CCC has employees and pays them on a weekly and monthly basis.	PAYE, NIC deductions need to be correct Data Protection regulations	Up to date payroll software ensuring accurate deductions and monthly reporting to HMRC. Personnel records should be securely maintained, either password protected or locked away.
CCC charges VAT on its invoices.	VAT regulations	Regular reporting of VAT to HMRC. Up to date accounting software to ensure that VAT is correctly calculated and accounted for on all transactions.
CCC charges interest on invoices paid late.	Late payment law as set out in the Late Payment of Commercial Debt (Interest) Act 1998	CCC should ensure that it complies with the rules regarding the charging of late payment interest. Credit control staff should be fully trained and kept up to date with changes in this legislation.
CCC is a private limited company exempt from audit.	Companies Act 2006 UK GAAP (or IFRS Standards)	CCC is a limited company and must adhere to the Companies Act 2006. It must prepare financial statements on an annual basis in line with UK GAAP (or IFRS Standards). The financial information should be accurate and timely and the directors need to ensure that the accounts are prepared in accordance with the Companies Act.

CHAPTER 2 The accounting function

Activity 1: Multitasking in a small organisation

As CCC is a small company with a small department of mainly part-time staff, it is difficult for it in its current process to ensure adequate controls and ensure supervision.

Stefan is in charge of the whole receivables process, from the raising of invoices through to the cash collection and the banking of monies. It would be not difficult for an individual in this capacity to 'skim' some of the receivable monies and write off any balance on the customer accounts.

Equally, as he opens the post alone, there is a risk that money may go missing, or be miscounted when it arrives in the post room.

A small organisation may lack the resources to effectively complete segregation of duties, but a director or another accounts clerk could act as a second signatory to confirm the money has arrived, or bank the money instead of Stefan.

Activity 2: Tall and flat organisation structures

(a) Advantages of the flat organisation structure for CCC:

- More freedom and responsibility for employees

- Quicker decision making by CCC that is not hindered by referring up many levels of management

- Quicker communication from top to bottom

- Less management cost

- Less bureaucracy

(b) Adding additional layers to the management structure at CCC could result in the following:

- More time for the directors to focus on the strategic and long-term plans for CCC rather than getting involved in the detailed day to day business of the company.

- Possible resentment from members of staff who like the flatter structure and do not want additional bureaucracy or increased controls in their working processes.

- A new level of management could provide additional controls, experience and management of the staff, especially where staff are mainly part time and there appears to be little 'hand over' or team spirit within the organisation.

- Many of the advantages outlined earlier would be lost eg more management cost in terms of salaries would result.

Activity 3: Culture

CCC

Smaller organisation, likely to be more teamwork as people will be expected to cover other employees' roles. The accounting department is small so, if the payroll clerk is on holiday, another employee who works on another part of the business would have to help out. Likely to be a more relaxed atmosphere based on the trust of individuals to report accurately their hours and to help out when needed.

NHS

Lots of levels of bureaucracy, likely to have more formalised rules and reporting structure. Rules and procedures are likely to be strongly adhered to, especially as their main role is regarding the health of the public.

Activity 4: Centralised accounting function

Advantages of CCC having a centralised accounting function:

- Greater economies of scale as fewer staff overall are needed to complete the same amount of work.

- Economies of scope as all departments benefit from having highly trained, expert accounting staff servicing their requirements.

- Consistency of approach as processes are only performed once.

- Standardised consistent procedures.

- Decisions can be made taking into account the 'big picture' eg the impact on the company as a whole.

- Major decisions on expenditure and investment such as recruitment can be centrally controlled.

Disadvantages of centralised accounting function:

- Analysis and decision making are remote from operational centres.

- There is little or no direct involvement with the rest of the company.

- It may lack relevant expertise if other departments are developing innovative business methods.

CCC is better suited to a centralised system so that all staff can be trained to use one system and can then cover each other's roles or access information if required. It will also enable financial reports to be quickly generated and easily provided to the joint owners for decision making.

Activity 5: Outsourcing

Payroll preparation/Human Resource management

- The experience of the payroll clerk is relatively limited and she has no HR experience.

- Issues may arise if an employee has a complex issue, such as long-term sickness, maternity pay or disciplinary procedures, all of which the current payroll clerk would struggle to deal with.

- There is a risk that the payroll methodology and calculation is not up to date as the clerk has not undertaken any further training since she qualified four years ago.

- Using a payroll bureau may be more expensive, but this will correct any errors made by the current staff as well as ensuring a strict segregation of duties in this high-risk area. Alternatively, a payroll bureau using up to date software and skilled staff may be able to perform these tasks in less time that Sonja takes, so may work out cheaper as well as better for CCC.

Financial statements and taxation preparation

- There are no fully qualified accountants in the team so accurate preparation of the financial statements and the taxation requirements may be beyond the capability of the current staff. Areas such as corporate taxation have complex requirements which means that CCC may be missing out on tax breaks or allowances, or filing returns incorrectly.

Legal advice

- There is minimal legal experience in the accounting department. This may become an issue for CCC if supplier or employee contracts need to be amended or legal issues arise, such as customer payment disputes or employee discrimination claims.

Activity 6: Sector analysis

Information type	Example(s)
Strategic	Forecast sales growth and market share.
	Profitability of the different types of product lines – carpet v vinyl.
	Capital structure and gearing analysis (the company is highly geared with the loan and overdraft).
	New stores to be opened in the region; who are the local competition, does the local economy suit a high-quality flooring sold at a premium price, or should it have a discounted store to sell on discontinued lines/offcuts?
	Consideration of independent and national competitors; there is little point in setting up a store next to a large, heavy-discounting national competitor.

Information type	Example(s)
Tactical	Resource utilisation such as: Sales per sales team member. Commission on a scale based on the type of product that CCC wants to focus on/launch new products, eg focusing on Umteeko products as they have better profit margins, so it makes tactical sense for the salespeople to focus on the products which have higher profit margins. Material wastage by product (can the flooring be cut in a more economical manner to minimise waste off cuts?). Customer satisfaction rating.
Operational	Staff timesheets and monitoring of efficiency and utilisation. Does every fitter manage to fit the same amount of flooring over a certain area, or are others better suited to more complex floorings? Customer ordering to delivery time. Individual customer feedback/customer satisfaction survey. Minimise the cost of waste by increasing recycling and minimising off cut wastage.

CHAPTER 3 Accounting systems

Activity 1: Flowchart of credit control

(a)

(b) Information which needs to be investigated further to ensure the flowchart is complete and to fully assess the accounting system for credit control:

- How are the debts chased by the team; are the customers phoned or letters written? Who is responsible for this role?

- Does management ever review the aged receivables report to decide whether any debts need to be classified as irrecoverable?

- What happens if the debt collection agency is unsuccessful?

- Can customers pay directly via BACS? How are these receipts identified and allocated to customers' accounts?

Activity 2: Documentation of controls

(a) Advantages of a user manual for CCC's accounting system:

- Quick and efficient training of new staff
- Better visibility of the controls in place
- Consistent approach to completing activities
- Easier to rotate staff between roles and responsibilities
- Easier to evaluate staff against standard procedures
- Improved supervisory and management control

(b) Disadvantages of a user manual:

- Increased risk of 'outsiders' being able to operate the system especially as the door to the accounting function is usually left open and the office unsecured.

- Procedures may stifle innovation and improvements to processes.

- User manuals take time to complete, and the accounting function at CCC is very short on resources currently, so this may take up too much time to the detriment of the day to day business.

- The manuals may become out of date quickly and a small company like CCC may not have time to regularly review and update the manuals.

- The manuals need to be tested to ensure they accurately reflect the systems in place.

- Staff often do not conform to manuals, negating the benefits of having them.

Activity 3: Security and IT at CCC

(a) The company might put in place the following rules regarding the use and control of passwords:

- Passwords must not be written down.

- Passwords must not be shared.

- Passwords must be changed regularly.

- Passwords must not be generic.

- When staff leave, access must be cancelled on the day they leave the company.

- Access can only be set up for new staff with management authorisation.

- Staff access to different parts of the system must be regularly reviewed.

(b) These rules and controls protect the integrity of the system and the company. If one password is used by all staff (generic) then there is little point in using them as the whole system is open to all. This lack of control then increases the risk of errors, from staff using parts of the system they are not trained to use, and fraud.

Access to the system should be controlled so that staff are not granted access to parts they do not require. If staff leave their access should be cancelled immediately so they cannot continue to use the system, and other staff cannot use their passwords. Often companies make sharing of passwords a disciplinary offence to ensure that controls are maintained.

(c) The policy states that only licensed software purchased by the company may be installed on company devices; however, the warehouse has two computers which have a personal version of software on them supplied by the warehouse manager.

There is no evidence of the payroll and purchase systems being regularly backed up, either to local backup devices or 'cloud' based support. It is not stated whether Stefan is using company-purchased hardware for the backup of the sales system or not. It is not evident that this is kept off site or locked away in the company safe in case of theft or fire.

Doors to the accounting department are kept open (even though there is a secure keypad-based lock) and the public can easily enter as the bathrooms are nearby.

Payroll is prepared in the same open area as the rest of the accounting function. There is a risk that secure and confidential information regarding staff salaries is open to access by other employees.

Activity 4: CCC accounting system

(a) The current IT system is Microsoft Office based and CCC does not use a bespoke or 'off the shelf' accounting system such as Sage. There are therefore no annual or monthly fees, making this a very cheap system to maintain.

However, most of the activities that the staff are required to do, such as raising invoices and preparing summary reports, take longer to complete because they use a Word template and this requires manual calculations.

Due to the manual nature of most of the transactions completed by staff, this can make the accounting system overly time consuming to update and use.

(b) Information is produced by the team when requested by management, apart from the quarterly reports set as standard (summary of financial revenue and expenses and a budgetary control report).

Although management have not yet noticed any issues regarding reliability of the IT system, the computers used by the staff are all 'stand-alone' and do not network. Therefore, the computers do not 'talk' to each other and information may be missed, or even duplicated. Currently only one member of staff actively backs up their data. There is a high risk that data may be lost if the computers crash. There is a risk that the information produced may be inconsistent with reporting requirements, for example, accuracy of the VAT and PAYE reporting due to the manual calculations involved.

(c) Given the manual element of the system, it takes longer and is more labour intensive to prepare internal reports, such as management accounts. The management accounts are only prepared quarterly for this reason, and it can take up to 20 days for them to be completed. Whilst this seems slow it may be entirely acceptable to the directors of CCC.

Overall: Although the current IT system costs little to maintain, it is not cost effective in terms of usage due to the manual nature of the processes undertaken by staff. This causes information output delays, and there is also a risk of data loss.

Activity 5: Ensuring ethical behaviour at work

Fundamental ethical principle	Explain how CCC may demonstrate these principles in practice
Integrity	The accounting function and system should be used to ensure information is accurate and not misleading. Staff should ensure that any issues regarding quality of data are raised immediately with management. The directors should ensure that financial statements are completed in a timely fashion.
Objectivity	Staff must not allow bias, conflict of interest or undue influence of others to override professional or business relationships.
Professional competence and due care	Ensure employees regularly update their technical knowledge, especially those with a responsibility for payroll, taxes and financial record keeping. Ensure regular monitoring of controls and processes by management and make adjustments when the business needs it or the organisation changes. Ensure all employees are aware of the health and safety regulations at work and that they attend any relevant courses. If staff do not feel that they can adequately complete a task, or are asked to do something which they do not feel able to do, then the issue should be raised with management and either an alternative resource should be found or training should be supplied.
Confidentiality	Security of payroll, supplier and customer data should be enhanced. Company business should not be discussed outside of the office or with third parties. Passwords should be used and data should be kept secured in locked cabinets and security of information at all times.

Fundamental ethical principle	Explain how CCC may demonstrate these principles in practice
Professional behaviour	Ensure staff remain professional and courteous to customers and suppliers and other employees.
	A culture should be built that enables staff to supply accurate and timely information to the best of their abilities.

Activity 6: Ethics conflict at CCC

(a) There is an **integrity** issue here alongside a **professional competence and due care** issue. Using averages instead of actual figures will almost certainly result in an inaccurate listing, and a report prepared without 'due care'.

Stefan should report the problem to Mr Cookridge and ask for an extension to the deadline in order to provide an accurate listing.

(b) There is a **confidentiality** issue here. Margaret needs the customer's authority to disclose the information; she may also need to confirm the identity of the person making the request. She should also take steps to protect the security of the information when she sends it: for example, not using email (which can be intercepted), and stating clearly that the information is confidential.

There is also a **professional behaviour** issue: to comply with the Data Protection Regulations it is likely that CCC has rules about what to do on receipt of such a request.

Margaret should not divulge any information without checking with a manager that she is legally allowed to do so.

(c) There are issues of **professional competence and due care** here. Stefan is not qualified to give advice on matters of taxation. Even if he were qualified, any answer he gives on the spot would risk being incomplete or inaccurate causing his friend tax losses. Stefan should advise his friend that he is unable to help, and point him in the direction of a qualified tax accountant.

(d) There is an **objectivity** issue here as the gift is of significant value. Think about how it looks: a third-party observer is entitled to wonder what 'special favours' deserve this extra reward – and/or how such a gift may bias Stefan when making payments to the supplier in future. Stefan should politely decline the offer, pointing out that he is merely doing his job.

Activity 1: The control environment

Within CCC controls are very informal. Reliance is often based on trust. Formal internal controls would support the accounting system and reduce the possibility of fraud occurring.

Petty cash – no control system is in place. People can help themselves to cash as and when needed; there is no control or reconciliation at the end of each day. Paula is no longer an employee and is still able to help herself to petty cash.

Cheques received in the post are not secured away in a locked drawer or a safe prior to sending to the bank.

Minimal segregation of duties – Stefan opens the post alone and logs the cheques into the day book without any checks or verifications in place.

Payroll controls are weak in that Sonja was able to make additional payments to Ron without any authorisation. She also did not verify the payment prior to making it in cash to Ron. There is also the potential that this was not documented, and there is no evidence Ron signed for the additional monies paid to him.

Health and safety regulations are not adhered to – an untrained person using a forklift without having the relevant training. This may be an issue if there was an accident as it is likely that CCC's insurance will be invalid.

The accounts receivable system is manual and there has been no regular review by management of the debt recovery process.

Activity 2: Sales controls (1) – Customers and orders

Control objective	Control activity	Risk and recommendations
Completeness of recording sales.	Sales orders are manually entered onto the system.	No pre-ordered invoice numbering, which allows for orders to be missed (customers taking goods without being invoiced). Manual system, open to error as the invoices are manually calculated on a Word template. Customer may be incorrectly invoiced, which could lead to loss of revenue or reputation if a customer is charged in error.

Control objective	Control activity	Risk and recommendations
		Recommendation: to buy an integrated accounting system with orders matching to invoices which are system calculated with pre-numbered invoices to ensure completeness.
Record invoices in the correct time period.	Implement cut-off procedure eg at the end of each month end review outstanding orders to make sure they are recorded in the correct month.	Invoices for new customers are not set up until the next month, so invoices are not recorded in the correct period. New customers should be set up prior to sales being authorised.
Only creditworthy customers are offered credit terms.	Credit checks on all orders over £200 to be completed at the point of sale.	Risk that CCC may incur financial losses due to not all customers being credit checked. Staff should be trained on how the checks are completed. Manager authorisation of all credit sales should be established to ensure that all sales with credit terms have been adequately checked. The unlimited credit line should be replaced with hard limits that can only be increased with the authority of the directors once a track record of reliable payment has been established.

Control objective	Control activity	Risk and recommendations
Record goods dispatched in the inventory system.	Inventory marked up for delivery and a dispatch note is manually raised.	Dispatch of goods should be authorised by appropriate personnel and checked to order documents.
		Dispatched goods should be checked for quality and quantity.
		Dispatch notes should be agreed to customer orders.
		Dispatch notes should be sequentially numbered and the sequence should be checked regularly.
		Inventory records should be updated from goods sent out records.
		Unfulfilled orders should be regularly reviewed.

Activity 3: Sales controls (2) – Credit control

Control objective	Control activity	Risk and Recommendations
Record all invoiced sales in the accounting records (sales ledger and general ledger).	Sales invoice sequence should be recorded and spoilt invoices recorded and destroyed.	Sales not recorded and wrongly omitted from financial statements.
		Payment not chased as the sale was never recorded.
		Regular reconciliations between sales invoices and sales ledgers required.

Control objective	Control activity	Risk and Recommendations
Record invoiced sales in the correct sales ledger accounts.	Receivables statements should be prepared and checked regularly; this is especially important with CCC as it has a manual system where invoices are input onto a spreadsheet, so the margin for error is greater. Receivables statements should be safeguarded so they cannot be amended before they are sent out (password protected). Accounts receivable control account should be reconciled regularly to the sales ledger.	Loss of custom by chasing the wrong customer for the debt. Not receiving the money from the correct customer. If the invoice is not entered onto the sales Excel spreadsheet then the debt may not get chased at all. This is one of the reasons CCC should consider a more integrated system.
Identify debts for which payment might be doubtful.	Overdue accounts should be reviewed and followed up. Regular review of the aged receivables report by staff and by management. Write-off of irrecoverable debts should be authorised by appropriate personnel.	Failure to take action until it is too late to recover the debt. Irrecoverable debts misstated as assets in the financial statements. Currently CCC has no regular review process for the aged receivables and no formalised method of reviewing the write-off of irrecoverable debts. Risk that valid and recoverable debts may be incorrectly written off.

Control objective	Control activity	Risk and Recommendations
Record all money received.	Supervise opening the post to avoid interception. There should be appropriate arrangements made when cashiers are on holiday. Receipts books should be serially numbered and kept locked up. Sales receipts should be matched with invoices. Customer remittance advices should be retained.	Money could be stolen or lost. Custom lost through chasing payments already made by the customer. Financial statements misstated. Risk that only one person opening the post and also recording any payments received may contribute to fraud or loss of cash or cheques (intentional or otherwise). Customers should be encouraged to pay via online banking or using cards in the shop.
Bank all money received.	Till rolls should be reconciled to cash collections which should then be agreed to cash banked. Cash and cheques should be banked daily. Paying in books should be compared to initial cash records. All receipts should be banked together. Where cards are taken in the shop, the card reader end of day report should reconcile to the card payments received in the till.	Money could be stolen or lost as banking is currently only completed twice a week. Custom lost through chasing payments already made by the customer. Financial statements misstated. Company cannot earn interest on money if it is not banked or pays additional overdraft interest.

Control objective	Control activity	Risk and Recommendations
Safeguard money received until it is banked.	There should be restrictions on who is allowed to accept cash (cashiers or salespeople). Cash received should be evidenced (till rolls, receipts). Cash registers should be regularly emptied. Cash shortages should be investigated. Opening of new bank accounts should be restricted to certain personnel and authorised by senior management. Cash floats held should be limited. Restrictions should be in place when making payments from cash received. Restrictions should be in place for access to cash on the premises. Cash floats should be checked by an independent person, sometimes on a surprise basis. Cash should be locked up outside normal business hours.	Money may be stolen in the interim period. Differences between the sales recorded in the tills and the cash actually received may go unnoticed and errors occur in the financial records. Banking should be more regular, and the company should consider only accepting payment via card to avoid cash-based risks altogether.

Activity 4: Purchases system controls

Take any four from the examples listed below.

Weakness	Control proposed	Risk controlled
Goods and services can be ordered for any purpose – personal or the company's benefit.	Necessity for orders should be evidenced before orders are authorised. Only prepare orders when purchase requisitions are received from relevant departments. Pre-number and safeguard blank order forms. Orders not yet received should be reviewed.	Company pays for unnecessary or personal goods.
Any suppliers can be used – no approved list.	Have a central policy for choosing suppliers. Monitor supplier terms and take advantage of discounts offered.	Unauthorised suppliers may not supply quality goods or may be too expensive. New suppliers may not offer credit terms, so cash flow is affected as the supplier must be paid prior to delivery.
No checks prior to inputting the invoice onto the Excel spreadsheet are completed back to the original order or the GRN.	Check invoices to purchase orders and GRNs to verify what was received.	Risk that invoices may not match what was ordered or what was received. Check invoices for prices, quantities and calculations.
Invoices are not logged when they arrive at CCC.	Reference invoices (stamp with sequential number and supplier reference). This will ensure that **all** invoices received go through the review and payment process.	Risk that invoices get missed when they arrive in the post. Company fails to pay for goods/services and loses suppliers.

Weakness	Control proposed	Risk controlled
Currently CCC only pays invoices at the end of the month.	The spreadsheet should detail the terms and conditions for the invoice, and any payment terms and whether any settlement or early discount can be taken. This would be significantly easier and be an automatic procedure if CCC had accounting software instead of a manual system.	Company may miss early settlement discounts or promotions, thus paying more for inventory.
There is no mention of how CCC can prevent paying a supplier twice. The spreadsheet does not appear to be updated once the payment has been made and there is a risk that cheques could be delayed in the post and a new one written if the supplier chases for payment.	Payments should be recorded promptly in the cash book and ledger. Propose that BACS payments (which are easily traceable and quicker) are used instead of cheques.	Company pays more than once and the supplier does not correct the mistake.
Goods are only checked for damage when they arrive; they are not verified to any order number.	Verify all incoming inventory back to a purchase order or purchase order listing (this may be manual in the case of CCC). Confirm that the inventory has been received and ensure the GRN is promptly sent to the accounts office (stamping the GRN with a sequential number so that the accounting team can see whether any GRNs are missing).	There is a risk that unordered, incorrect or wrong goods are accepted upon delivery.

Weakness	Control proposed	Risk controlled
Cheques are the only method provided for CCC paying its suppliers. This can delay payment if the signatory is not available leading to the use of pre-signed cheques.	Cheques should be requisitioned and requests evidenced with supporting documentation. Cheque payments should be authorised by someone other than a signatory. Cheques should never be signed before the amount and the payee are completed. Signed cheques should be dispatched promptly.	Only make payments to the correct recipients and for the correct amounts which are authorised.
Purchase orders are not ticked off by the accounting team, so they are not aware of what invoices they are expecting. Equally, GRNs are not verified and checked against invoices received on a systematic basis. There is a risk that goods may have arrived but not be invoiced (accrual at year end missing) or an invoice has been received but no goods (in which case, the invoice should not be paid until receipt).	Purchase order listing should be regularly reviewed and any missing orders chased up. GRNs should be matched to orders and invoices matched to GRNs. GRNs should be verified and checked against invoices received on a systematic basis.	Financial statements may be misstated by recording a purchase but not inventory, or recording inventory but not the associated liability. Penalty from HMRC for recording VAT in the wrong VAT period.

Activity 5: CCC – Payroll controls

Payroll control in place	Control weakness	Suggested control to be introduced
Cash is kept in the petty cash tin and locked in the safe at night. Cash wages are kept in the safe once calculated. They are handed to the manager for distribution (see weakness).	The use of cash to pay wages could lead to the payroll staff colluding with weekly staff and adding more cash to the pay packet than the amount earned or shown on the wages slip. Although wages should be handed out by the manager this can be overridden if he is busy.	BACS payments to be introduced for all staff to ensure only fully validated amounts are received by staff (and fully traceable if there is a dispute). Cash wages should cease. Payslips could be posted to the home address. If cash wages retained: Identity of staff should be verified before payment (with wages being signed out by staff). Distributions of cash wages should be recorded.
Staff rotas with details of hours worked are sent by the managers to the payroll clerk.	Gross pay is calculated manually, which increases the risk of errors. There is no verification of when staff start or finish, as no time records are kept.	Introduce a payroll system which calculates gross pay based on hours worked instead of manual calculation. Regular checks should be carried out of the payroll records against the HR records and vice versa. If retaining manual system, ensure that another member of staff verifies the calculation.

Payroll control in place	Control weakness	Suggested control to be introduced
Payroll clerk counts out the cash and draws up the BACS listing.	Errors can occur or additional amounts be added to the cash wages.	Segregation of duty of the calculation and payment of wages and salaries. BACS payments should be verified by management once set up on the system by the payroll clerk; however, they only agree to the calculation (the calculation is not verified). Bank transfer lists should be prepared and authorised. Bank transfer lists should be compared to the payroll.
Deductions are calculated by payroll clerk using tax tables.	Errors can occur and incorrect deductions possibly made. Risk that incorrect submissions are made to HMRC.	Ensure all deductions have been properly calculated and authorised. Consider outsourcing to a payroll bureau, or using approved HMRC software to comply with RTI requirements.

Activity 6: SWOT analysis

Strengths	Weaknesses
• An open plan accounts office ensures that when staff are in and working with each other they can communicate freely and cover each other's work when absent. • The cheque book is kept in a locked desk in the office – but see weaknesses. • A credit reference agency is used to decide whether to grant credit. • Some credit control procedures are in place. • Controls re: cash and cheques coming into the office involve a manual day book then accounts.	• As most accounts staff are part time there are often occasions when no one is in the office. The door is generally propped open; there is a risk members of the public could access the office. • As all staff can access the office and the accounting system with common passwords, there is a lack of control. There will also be issues concerning communication between staff as they are not all in the office at the same time. • Stand-alone computers, with no central system or database, reduces the ability to produce meaningful reports for key stakeholders. Risk of loss of data if a computer fails.

Strengths	Weaknesses
• Staff seem keen to improve systems – the Accounts Receivable Clerk has implemented some initiatives. • Cash movement is reduced by using cash to make up wages.	• Staff as a whole are not qualified in accounting, which poses a risk of errors, exacerbated by the relaxed controls and also a lack of accountability. • Office staff are paid by cheque – the frequent use of cheques can lead to the risk of cheques being stolen and fraudulently used. • Manual calculation of weekly payroll with no secondary check is a weakness as it can lead to errors or fraudulent increases in staff pay. • Wages are paid in cash – any use of cash poses a risk of theft. • Overdue debts are often not followed up beyond an initial phone call. • The cheque book is kept in an easily accessible drawer which is sometimes left unlocked. • Staff are not trained in Excel, increasing the risk of errors. • Invoices are produced using Word – this has potential for errors, such as duplication of invoice number or incorrectly calculated. • Cash is not counted when removed from the tills on weekdays. • No controls over petty cash and over cash taken from tills. • No contingency planning – accounting staff are not able to take on each other's roles when absent. • Staff are unable to cover each other's roles as they lack the skills to do so. • No control on authorisation – signing of blank cheques to cover absence. • No controls on payments to suppliers or payments from customers. • Payments to suppliers are made without checking systems or informing other staff.

Strengths	Weaknesses
	• Lack of controls on staff hours may lead to incorrect rotas and staff pay. • Pay packets for more than one pay period can be stored onsite – this is a weakness as too much cash is in the office.

Opportunities	Threats
• There is an opportunity to use one central accounting system on networked computers, which will ensure there is better cover for work when staff are absent and better reporting of key financial information to relevant stakeholders. • There is an opportunity to train staff in accounting and also in the systems they use, making them much more aware of the controls and procedures they should be operating and also more efficient. • There is an opportunity to train staff in each other's roles – perhaps with a backup member of staff for each. This could motivate staff and also ensure cover during absence. • There is an opportunity to re-outsource the payroll function to the company accountants.	• Using spreadsheet software (Excel) to prepare accounts poses a risk of errors being made in formulas that are difficult to spot, resulting in incorrect inventory and accounting information. • The use of one common password is a threat to systems and the data held within them (for example through unauthorised access). • The lack of formal procedures and controls has contributed to extensive use of the overdraft facility and caused the bank concern. This is a cash flow threat to the company. • There appears to be no backup taken of the current systems. This is a threat because key financial data would be lost if the systems failed. • Regulatory environment – this is constantly changing, for example potential changes to VAT rates. The accounting system needs to be able to recognise these changes and react accordingly. • Debt collection – while a relationship with a debt collection agency is in place, this is rarely used due to the costs involved. This may mean that debts are never recovered.

CHAPTER 5 Monitoring controls and detecting fraud

Activity 1: Potential frauds at CCC

Frauds that could occur within the accounting system could include the following (note that this list is not exhaustive):

	Potential fraud
Purchases and inventory	• Theft of assets – computers or other assets could be stolen by any of the staff within CCC due to the easy access to the accounts office.
	• Theft of inventory – there is no mention of controls such as inventory counts to prevent the theft of inventory from the warehouse. The Excel spreadsheet used to record movements of, or changes to the level of, inventory is also an ineffective control as staff fail to update it.
	• Overpayment of supplier invoices – there is no control to check that cheques prepared to pay suppliers equate to the amount owed and invoiced.
Payroll	• Overstatement of wages – there are no controls in place to approve actual wages paid to staff, so the Wages Clerk could overstate wages by either overpaying on hours worked and/or the hourly rate.
	• Overstatement of hours worked – the stores supervisor could add more hours to the staff rotas than physically worked by staff.
	• Monetary theft via the setting up of a ghost employee – there are no controls over the addition of new starters to the payroll system, such as a requirement for documentation that cannot be overridden, segregation of duties, or linking to HR records. This means that a person could set up a fictional employee and keep the wages 'earned' for themselves.

	Potential fraud
Bank and cash	• Theft of cheques – there are few controls in place to store the cheque book securely, and it has been found in an unlocked drawer together with blank, signed cheques. • Theft of cash from the office – petty cash is kept in the staff room and there is little control over access to the office. There is no one member of staff responsible for the petty cash tin and the only control is a sheet on which any expenses paid for using petty cash should be logged. However, this control is currently ineffective as it would appear that it is not being used. Staff have also been borrowing money from this tin on occasions. There are frequently discrepancies between the amount that should be in the tin and surprise at finding the tin empty or running low. • Theft of cash or cheques from the mail – no separate controls are in place to record cash and/or cheques received. • Theft of cash and/or cheques from tills – the tills are not balanced each evening so there is no accountability for any missing cash and/or cheques.
Sales and aged receivables system	• Under-recording of goods sold – there are few controls in place to ensure goods purchased are accurately recorded. • Writing off debts – there are no controls to ensure that debts from customers are not written off, or to ensure that they are written off when they should be.

Activity 2: Sales system fraud

(a)

Fraud which could occur at CCC	Why this risk has arisen
Stolen cash receipts through the non-reconciliation of the till records and the cash inside them	The risk is increased by leaving the tills full of cash overnight. Any error or shortfall will not be detected until the next day or when the staff come to reconcile the takings. Having significant amounts of cash on the premises increases the threat of theft or loss.
No credit cheques undertaken against B Braithwaite	It's potential fraud risk as the customer may buy items on credit with no intention of paying (theft of inventory) or the customer may be a fictitious one set up by an unscrupulous member of the sales team who wants to inflate their sales figures for commission payments.
Overcharging on sales	It is possible that customers are being overcharged and sales staff are skimming off the excess monies being charged.
Writing off debts	All debts require management authorisation to be written off. Currently debts are written off as and when Stefan believes that they cannot be collected or they have got 'just too old'.

(b) Without management or senior staff performing regular reviews of the aged receivables ledger, the following issues may occur:

Financial loss

The unallocated cash does not show what debts or final balances need to be settled by customers. By delaying the allocation of cash, it is possible that fraud could occur by 'teeming and lading' (cash receipts being skimmed off and then applying other customer receipts to cover it. By delaying the overall outstanding debt this type of fraud may only appear if another person performs a reconciliation of the ledger or the customers are contacted directly).

Financial loss due to staff inflating the sales figures and earning more commission.

Financial loss due to inflated sales and risk of overstating VAT liability.

Non-financial

The high level of unallocated cash suggests that customers' invoices may appear to be outstanding when they have, in fact, paid. This could adversely affect customer relations if they are chased for debts that they have settled in full.

Equally, with the cheques being dropped and lost when they are received in the post, the risk of paid debts being chased will affect customer relations.

If fraud has occurred, then staff morale may drop due to a climate of suspicion.

Activity 3: Purchases system fraud

Ordering goods for own use – there are issues around segregation of duties between ordering, booking goods into inventory and payments, plus appropriate authorisations. Management should authorise all purchase orders, so that all orders placed can be verified and there are no 'surprises' in value or in finding that staff are using company funds to purchase goods for personal use.

The potential for fictitious suppliers – there should be management authorisation of all new suppliers added to the system; reconciliation of payments to invoices; and some segregation of duties for these processes. The new suppliers may all be valid, but management should also be reviewing whether they represent best value in terms of price, quality and credit terms offered.

Invoices incorrectly calculated – CCC may have paid the incorrect amount of £15,000 if this had not been such a significant error and investigated further. Suitable controls would be to match goods received to purchases orders, then matching the invoice to the purchase order when it arrives to check that the supplier has correctly calculated the quantities and prices.

Time wasted – it took Margaret all day to reconcile the manual system to find out what had happened with the incorrectly calculated invoice. If there was a fully integrated system, this would have been highlighted much sooner and any investigation would have taken significantly less time.

By delaying the payment to the supplier, and not raising the issue earlier, CCC has risked affecting the relationship with this supplier.

Cash flow effect – working capital would have been significantly affected if this £15,000 invoice had been paid, and there is the potential for strained relations with the bank if CCC had asked for an extension to its bank overdraft. Any request to increase the overdraft will result in higher interest charges, as well as possible arrangement fees.

Activity 4: Payroll risks

To: The Directors of CCC
Risk assessment of the payroll system based on events in October 20X2

There is a high risk of errors in the payroll system due to:

- Unauthorised additional payments to staff taking place.

- Sales commission not being checked by a member of management (for example, the sales manager) prior to payment.

- New starters being put onto the system without any documentation or checks documented regarding their hours, contract and terms and conditions, or whether they actually exist.

- Large amounts of cash kept on the premises with staff being able to top up wages by taking £1,200 out of petty cash without any safeguards, checks or authorisation in place.

- There being no controls over the hours and rates that staff are being paid. There is a risk that these could be amended resulting in staff being paid too much.

Risk of regulatory failure due to:

- New starters being paid on the system prior to the tax information being received. There is a risk that their deductions will be incorrect, risking penalties from HMRC or complaints from staff affected.

- Spoilt payslips being thrown away and not correctly destroyed; this is a confidentiality risk and puts the company at risk of breach of Data Protection regulations.

- The payroll clerk has had no further training since she qualified four years ago. There is no mention of what qualification she currently has or any required continuing professional development. It is possible that new regulations are missed and the company may be fined eg there is no pension scheme despite this being a legal requirement for all employers in the UK.

- No checks on proof of identity are made, or references required when new staff members join. This could expose the company to risk of theft as well as breaches of Money Laundering regulations.

Risk of ethical breaches occurring in the workplace due to:

- Bullying and intimidation of payroll staff by members of the sales team – see Ron's treatment of Sonja. All staff should be treated with respect; aggressive and threatening behaviour should not be tolerated.

- Breach of confidentiality by leaving spoilt payslips with employee information in the bin rather than being destroyed.

Activity 5: Detecting fraud using financial information

- **Irrecoverable debts** – have increased by 175% (whereas revenue has increased by 19%). This suggests that there may be issues regarding the collection of cash or screening of customers (from Activity 2 we know B. Braithwaite was added with no credit checks). However, from a detection of fraud basis, this could also suggest that cash is being collected from customers and these debts are being written off rather than the cash being applied to them (there was lots of unallocated cash in the most recent aged receivable report). Irrecoverable debts which are written off should also be authorised by a member of management. Management should review a list of the debts (one of the directors last looked at it four months ago) to be written off with explanations as to why this is the case and steps taken to recover any outstanding debt.

- **Sales staff salaries** – have increased by 75% which, given the rise of revenue by 19%, is odd. There had been a case of one of the sales staff requesting additional commission and this being paid without being checked. This is a potential area of fraud. Sales commission should be reviewed by the directors prior to being paid. Management should be able to review the sales made by the member of staff (including any credits or refunds given). In order to ensure that credit notes are not being raised after the invoice in order to 'boost' sales, the commission should only be paid after a predetermined period of time (eg quarterly intervals) to allow cut-off testing to be performed.

- **Other costs** – management should ensure they understand what drives these costs so that they do not simply 'creep up' over time, as many of these should be fixed in nature.

- **Other factors which may be considered**
    - Ensuring that the management accounts are regularly reviewed by the management team
    - Monthly management accounts rather than quarterly would help to highlight any problems most quickly
    - Looking at the actual results against budget to see if the company is 'on track' and the accounts look reasonable

Activity 6: CCC budget control report

(a) Areas of focus

The sales team appear to be exceeding expectations by selling more product and at a better price than budgeted. However, Stefan should highlight the adverse variances in respect of material usage and labour efficiency.

There may be issues with the budgetary process in calculating how much product is required – for example, a customer may want a 25 m² room covered with a given product but this may require more than 25 m² of flooring depending on the shape of the room. From the analysis the adverse material usage indicates that either the fitters are using too much product during the fitting process, or the budget itself is not allowing for realistic levels of wastage eg offcuts.

The adverse labour efficiency ratio may be related to this. The pre-seen information has highlighted an issue with the lack of fitting time allocated to the Umteeko product. The budget may need to be revised and the sales price amended upwards to reflect the additional time and procedures in fitting this specialist product.

(b) Limitations

The budgetary control report does not show the absorption of fixed costs, which is vital in terms of pricing, as the price charged must cover both direct and indirect costs if a business is to be profitable. If the fixed costs such as rent are not priced into the budget report, then the directors will not fully understand why they are making losses or very small overall profits.

Only a certain number of products are currently being monitored due to the limitations of the system (Excel based) and the limited time, experience and judgement of Stefan.

By only selecting a few products, it does not help the directors to fully understand why CCC is struggling financially.

Activity 7: Balanced scorecard and ratios

The directors of CCC may wish to consider some of the following useful ratios and indicators for success to monitor the company's success in respect of the objectives set by John Cookridge.

(a) Financial success

Gross profit percentage $\dfrac{\text{Gross profit}}{\text{Re venue}} \times 100\%$

	31.12.X2	31.12.X1
Gross profit percentage	$\dfrac{403}{1,106} \times 100\% = 36\%$	$\dfrac{297}{930} \times 100\% = 32\%$
Carpets	$\dfrac{92}{379} \times 100\% = 24\%$	$\dfrac{143}{425} \times 100\% = 34\%$
Vinyl	$\dfrac{311}{727} \times 100\% = 43\%$	$\dfrac{154}{505} \times 100\% = 30\%$

The gross profit of CCC has increased year on year based upon the financial statements. Using the information available in the extract from the management accounts for the same periods, it is clear that the vinyl side of the business is more profitable (for 20X2, carpets made a gross profit percentage of 24% compared to that of vinyl of 43%). This is potentially down to the success of the Umteeko product.

The profitability of vinyl has increased by 13% since the prior year (which had no Umteeko business).

It would be useful for the directors to understand in more detail which product lines in the vinyl business are making the highest profits, and whether any of the carpet lines are unprofitable and need to be retired. This can only be analysed by a more detailed analysis of the profitability of each product line.

Another useful ratio which can be calculated is the operation profit percentage, as this will reveal the extent to which the company is controlling its indirect costs.

- Operating profit percentage $\dfrac{\text{Profit from operations}}{\text{Revenue}} \times 100\%$

(b) Customer satisfaction

Currently CCC has no way of monitoring customer satisfaction (based on the information available). Recommended options may include:

- Analysing the number of repeat customers over a certain period

- Undertaking a customer satisfaction survey

- Logging the number of customer complaints and the nature of them (quality of product, fitting service and staff professionalism)

(c) Process efficiency

Cash flow can be monitored using a series of liquidity and working capital ratios.

For example:

		31.12.X2	31.12.X1
Accounts payable days	$\dfrac{\text{Trade payables}}{\text{Cost of sales}} \times 365$ days	68 days	49 days
Working capital cycle	Inventory days + Receivables days – Payable days	44 + 44 – 68 = 20 days	35 + 33 – 49 = 19 days
Quick (acid) test	$\dfrac{\text{Current assets} - \text{Inventories}}{\text{Current liabilities}} = X{:}1$	0.78:1	0.52:1

The **accounts payable days** shows that CCC is taking much longer to pay its suppliers, and as these are over 68 days (with the usual business terms of credit being 28 days) this is a worrying sign and should flag up to the directors that there is a problem. It may be that the invoices are not being paid until CCC staff are chased for payment (which is not good for supplier relations and goes against the ethical treatment towards suppliers as set out in the company mission statement). CCC may lose credit status with suppliers, and therefore have to pay for inventory up front – known as 'proforma invoicing' – or lose that supplier altogether. The directors will need to understand whether this is a systematic failure across the whole of accounts payable or whether just one or two large (and disputed) invoices are causing the ratio to be distorted.

The **working capital cycle** is short, which is good news, as it lowers the amount of money tied up in the business. However, below the headline figures there are potentially problems arising with the receivables – as these have increased from 33 to 44 days. Again, the directors need to focus on why this is happening, and what action should be taken to prevent a cash flow crisis.

The acid test proves what the earlier two ratios have already highlighted. As the ratio is less than 1:1 it highlights that the current assets are not sufficient to pay the suppliers (or other current liabilities) at that current time. Although the ratio is improving, there are still significant issues for the directors to investigate.

(d) Growth

CCC should undertake an analysis of what training has been undertaken by its staff and consider whether this is sufficient for their needs. Only Stefan is undertaking any current accountancy training and there are only two Umteeko trained fitters. As CCC intends to use its success in the Umteeko product to expand its business, it should consider expanding the level of training to other fitters, especially those trained only on carpets, as this is a shrinking market.

Currently CCC has no further data on what the competition is doing in terms of other local independent flooring companies. Analysis into the local competition and monitoring of the growth of national firms in the local area would aid CCC's strategic planning, especially if it is planning to open new stores in the region.

Activity 8: Fraud matrix CCC

This fraud matrix suggests improvements to the controls CCC currently has in place. They have to be appropriate to the company; we could not suggest full segregation of duties within CCC as there are not enough staff working within the accounting function to make this possible. Also, the assessment of risk is subjective, based on our knowledge of the company and the controls currently in place.

Potential fraud	Controls currently in place	Risk to CCC 1 = low, 5 = high	Implications/ Regulations affected
Theft of assets	Physical access to the accounting function controlled by keypad but with common entry code, and door left propped open.	2	Loss of assets such as computers and possibly key data and information. Financial loss.

Potential fraud	Controls currently in place	Risk to CCC 1 = low, 5 = high	Implications/ Regulations affected
Overstatement of wages – Wages Clerk Additional monies being paid to staff without the formal support of payroll records	None	4	Overpayment of wages to staff. Financial loss.
Theft of cash from the office	Petty cash is kept in the staff room and office has keypad access, but is left propped open. Contains notebook for recording expenses charged to petty cash, but this control is often not followed.	3	Loss of cash.
Theft of cheques	Cheque book kept in locked drawer – but control not always followed.	4	Cheques could be used for own purchase/ cash. Financial loss.
Overstatement of hours worked – showroom supervisor	None	3	Overpayment of wages to showroom staff.
Theft of inventory from warehouse	An Excel spreadsheet showing inventory levels and location of inventory is in place; however, this document is not always updated and inventory checks back to it do not tend to occur.	4	Loss of inventory.

Potential fraud	Controls currently in place	Risk to CCC 1 = low, 5 = high	Implications/ Regulations affected
Fictitious suppliers could be entered onto the system and payments made	None	4	Financial loss.
Overpayment of supplier invoices	None	3	Increased costs. Financial loss.
Under-recording of goods sold	None	3	Reduced revenue.
Writing off customer debts without authorisation	None	3	Financial loss risk due to monies which are recovered being misappropriated whilst the debt is wrongly written off. Reputational risk as customer will be unhappy by the chasing of an already paid debt.
Theft of cash/ cheques from the mail	Cash and cheques received are written into day book by the same person who opens the post. There is no segregation of duty here; it would be better for Stefan to wait until another member of staff is present to witness the opening of post.	2	Lost cash/ cheques, reduced revenue. Reputational risk as customer will be unhappy by the chasing of an already paid debt.
Theft of cash/ cheques from the tills	None – tills are not reconciled until the following day.	3	Lost cash/ cheques.

Potential fraud	Controls currently in place	Risk to CCC 1 = low, 5 = high	Implications/ Regulations affected
Theft of wages arising from the payment to a ghost employee	Documentary evidence should be provided before any new starter can be set up on the payroll system; however, there is evidence that this is not always the case.	3	Lost cash/ increased costs.
Disclosure of staff information without the proper authority	None	3	Potential fine or penalties caused by breach of the Data Protection Regulations.
Peter Cookridge buying inventory higher than usual to benefit personally from the supplier who will support his motorcycling	None	4	Cash flow issues. Too high an inventory level (affecting working capital). Financial loss. Potential breach of the Bribery Act 2010.

CHAPTER 6 Making changes to systems

Activity 1: Business regulations

(a) Potential weaknesses

- Lack of qualified accountancy staff and no evidence of ongoing professional development from the payroll clerk suggest that CCC may not be aware of any accounting or payroll developments. Evidence suggests that CCC may already be in breach of the requirement to provide a pension to staff (although it is not explicit that CCC has breached any deadline).

- There does not appear to be any nominated officer (in line with money laundering regulations) within CCC. It is doubtful that all of the regulations are being followed correctly and staff have no central point to discuss any concerns in this area.

- There is no evidence of health and safety checks; this may be an issue with the company insurance if there is an accident at work.

- Data Protection breaches have already been identified, but staff have not been trained in this area so further breaches are likely to occur.

(b) Recommendations

- Ensure that management review the training of staff regarding companies regulations especially in money laundering, health and safety etc.

- Designate different members of staff to become the 'champions' in those areas, providing training and ensuring that these members of staff take the time to inform the rest of the team. This should also improve morale as the staff will feel motivated that CCC is investing in their training and valuing their input on these important areas.

- Ensure that Stefan, Sonja and any new accountancy staff regularly attend update courses and request that they report back on any new developments to the management team so that they have a view of what systems or processes may need to be amended at the earliest opportunity.

Activity 2: Tangible cost of a new system

(a) The tangible costs associated with the new system might include:

- Cost of staff time – preparing the data for migration to the new system and assisting the software contractors.

- The cost of the 'learning curve' whereby staff will be slower initially on the new software whilst they practise using it. There may initially be teething problems eg being able to use the reports and understanding what the system can and cannot do.

- Customer dissatisfaction at potential shop closure, or restricted access to staff during the period of transition and training.

(b) Cost of implementing the new system:

Full system initial cost   £10,800
Annual ongoing cost   £5,800

These costs would be reduced if CCC decides not to go ahead with all of the add-on; however, having an integrated system would lead to reduced calculation errors, simpler and faster online reporting (to HM Revenue & Customs for PAYE) and closer monitoring of the inventory chain.

- Initial training costs will be dependent on how many staff will be trained. If at least ten staff members (including both directors) are trained, it would be cost effective to have an in-house training programme. The financial outlay would be the same as sending all ten to college, but it would reduce the travel expenses.

- The downside would be that ten people would be unavailable to perform business work on the day of training.

- CCC may consider to send selected members of staff to college to complete the learning, for example five staff members costing £350 each, total cost of £1,750, and these staff could act as 'champions' and assist those members of staff who will complete the online training (such as more restricted users, maybe in the warehouse).

The training programme selected will need to be considered in terms of the financial costs, plus the opportunity costs of staff being unavailable to process orders to secure sales.

Activity 3: Intangible costs

Intangible costs might include:

- Staff discontent amongst those not chosen to receive training on the new system. Additionally some staff may get different levels of training, such as some going to college for the course and others completing the online course. This may lower staff morale and productivity.

- Staff completing the online course; there is a risk that they will not complete the training in line with the launch of the new system. The licence allows six months' access, so staff using the online training will need to be reviewed to ensure they have completed it on time, and are not wasting time surfing the internet.

Activity 4: Benefits of training

Intangible benefits might include:

- Staff are better trained in basic knowledge and skills so they are more efficient.

- Staff morale improves as they feel valued due to the investment in training them, increasing their motivation.

- Customers see well-trained and knowledgeable staff so the company's reputation is enhanced, leading to more repeat custom and recommendations from satisfied customers.

- If everyone is trained at the same time (such as using the in-house training), staff can discuss issues with each other rather than struggling on alone. It will act as a team building exercise and improve morale.

Activity 5: Cost-benefit analysis

A cost-benefit analysis of the recommendation to implement a centralised, integrated accounting system, and to train staff appropriately on it, has been completed as follows:

To: The Directors of CCC Ltd

Date: 23 April 20X3

Cost-benefit analysis on the proposed implementation of the KashCade system and staff training.

	£	£
Initial costs		
Initial installation & set up	5,000	
First year's licence (550 + 3,250 + 750 + 1,250)	5,800	
Training costs (2 day option)	3,500	
Disruption to sales and accounts department (£540 × 2) + sales department (£2,000 × 2)	5,080	
Consultant cost	750	
		20,130
Ongoing costs		
Support system (4 × £250)	1,000	
Annual licence (4 × £5,800)	23,200	
		24,200
Total costs		**44,330**
Savings		
Efficiencies due to new system £6,300 × 5		31,500
Increase in revenue/savings due to reduced inventory holding. (5,000 + 5,750 + 6,612 + 7,604 + 8,745)		33,711
Total savings		**65,211**
Total benefit		**20,881**

Costs

Set-up and annual system costs

An example of a system that would suit CCC's needs is a centralised accounting software package, such as KashCade in this example, which has been specifically created for small to medium-sized businesses. There are many similar packages on the market and a full investigation should be completed to determine which best suits the company. A reputable, proven package with a multi-user licence would cost approximately £10,800 (including the initial set-up costs of £5,000 and the first year's licence of £5,800). The basis for choosing the package should include ease of use (for example drop-down menus), the help facility and the user manuals. The ongoing annual cost for licences will be £5,800 per year (£3,250 + £550 + £750 + £1,250), although there may be increases in future years due to inflation or upgrades in the level of cover required by CCC.

Support package costs

CCC would also need to purchase an appropriate support package to ensure users have access to trained support professionals and that software upgrades and bug fixes are received. An estimated cost for this is an additional £250 per year, although Kashcade have included the first year free of charge.

Training for staff cost

Appropriate training for staff is required. If the accounting package purchased is one in common use then CCC will be able to purchase places on open courses for staff, costing approximately £350 per staff member. CCC might also consider a tailored training course for all staff at once, to include partial set-up of the system for CCC's use, which would cost approximately £3,500 and staff would be trained over two days minimising disruption to the business. Costs of replacement staff in the accounts department would be £540 per day (totalling £1,080).

There would be an opportunity cost when staff attend the training in that they would not be available to complete their work at CCC while they are on the course. This would be shown as potential lost revenue of £2,000 per day from the sales staff (totalling £4,000).

Hardware and infrastructure cost

The company requires the appropriate equipment to network the computers. This could be completed either by cable or on a secure wireless network, and would have a cost. Cabling would be more reliable but would create disruption to the office while being installed, whereas a wireless network would be less disruptive to install but may be less reliable.

A cloud-based system such as KashCade will not require much in the way of installing the actual software, but it is important to verify that the broadband speed and existing computer capacity are compatible with the requirements of the system. There may be an additional requirement to upgrade hardware or to buy new terminals for the warehouse or sales staff. Currently CCC only has four computers, so more will need to be purchased at a cost for the warehouse and sales staff and directors' access.

Transition costs

CCC would face some disruption while the new accounting system is installed and set up. CCC may need to pay for additional staff time to enter data for customers, suppliers and employees into the system so that it is fully operational, and it is anticipated that this could be completed within one week. This would potentially require an additional week of paid hours.

A further cost the company should consider, but one that is harder to quantify, is staff discontent at a change to the current system. Staff within the accounting team may be unhappy about needing to learn new working practices, increased controls and how to operate a new system. Other employees may see the increased controls in place as preventing them from carrying out their work, and unnecessary.

Procedure manuals cost

There would be a cost associated with producing procedure manuals to ensure staff know the expected working practices and procedures surrounding the new accounting system. There should also be a rota produced for cover when staff are absent. This should be completed by the Senior Accounts Clerk, as part of their normal role. As an estimate, this would take approximately 20 hours of their time per year.

Benefits

Increased information benefit

The first benefit to CCC would be the ability to produce reports from the centralised accounting system that provide complete information showing the full financial position of the company. These reports can be reviewed on a regular basis by both the directors and the Senior Accounts Clerk. The cash-related reports should help ensure cash flows are effectively managed. This will benefit the company by reducing overdraft fees and avoiding embarrassment with suppliers. The reports produced would include:

- Statement of profit or loss
- Statement of financial position
- Statement of cash flows
- Aged receivable analysis
- Cash flow forecast
- Supplier payment reports
- Costs by cost centre/code
- Analysis of petty cash expenditure
- Payroll reports
- Budgets and budgetary control reports

The financial statements could be prepared in draft format by the accounting team, reducing the input by the external accountancy firm, with a longer-term view to bringing the preparation of the financial statements in-house completely.

Cash flow benefits

An aged receivable analysis can be produced to strengthen the system of chasing overdue debts and ensure customers who have not paid are put on stop quickly. This will prevent customers from taking advantage of the current lax controls.

Cash flow forecasts will enable the directors and the Senior Accounts Clerk to estimate the cash inflows to and outflows from the company, manage cash balances more effectively and reduce the overdraft and related fees. It will also assist with the planning of any significant cash expenditure. Overdraft fees and interest payments could be reduced each year.

Payroll security, accuracy and efficiency

The payroll will be accurately produced when required, with the benefit of the system being up to date on payroll rules and regulations such as tax rates. This will produce a benefit of more accuracy, fewer queries and increased efficiency of staff time, as well as compliance with RTI. It is estimated that the system will speed up the completion of the payroll each month. As HM Revenue & Customs requires monthly online payroll reporting, this will ensure that the process is made more efficient as Sonja does not need to type the monthly totals into the system (they will already be there and the software sends the information once it is ready and authorised for transmission).

Disaster recovery

There will be less danger from a system breakdown with appropriate backup of a central system. If one computer were to fail then the other staff could continue working, and a support agreement would ensure that if the main system failed it could be operational again as quickly as possible with less risk of lost or corrupted data. Holding the data in the 'cloud' as KashCade's system does will ensure that upgrades are completed by KashCade rather than a member of the team at CCC having to install the necessary information.

Supplier relations

Another benefit would be improved supplier relations, as suppliers should be paid the correct amounts and on time. This could also benefit the credit terms and conditions that suppliers grant CCC, further improving cash flow.

If the suppliers offer prompt payment (settlement) discounts, these could be monitored and utilised by CCC thus making additional cost savings.

Fraud

Further benefits are the significant reduction in the risk of fraud and the improvement of controls within the system together with improved cost control. Central reports will assist both the owners and the Senior Accounts Clerk with analysing payments and wages and identifying where costs are higher than expected. Due to current poor controls, it is not known if CCC has suffered from fraudulent activities, so benefits are hard to evaluate.

Morale

Another benefit is the improved morale of staff. The accounting team would benefit from training, including formal accounting training as requested, and this would improve their efficiency and effectiveness as well as morale. Better-motivated staff should result in lower staff turnover and also improved commitment to the company.

The morale of the non-accounting staff will be improved by the timely completion of accurate wages.

Regulations

A final benefit is that CCC will be able to comply with regulations such as the Data Protection Regulations with good, secure storage of its data and information. Payroll reporting will be automated and can be completed on time, and VAT returns (if appropriate) can be automatically calculated and sent to HM Revenue & Customs.

Activity 6: Issues during transition

Accounting system introduction

- Training staff, cost and fear of new system especially by some members of the team, such as warehouse staff who may have had limited exposure to computerised inventory systems in the past (the current system is based on Excel).

- Data loss during migration to the new system or moving data which is incorrect across to the new package. It is important to ensure that data moved onto the new system is correct and accurate. Customer and supplier details should be checked and balances verified. This will take time, but it must be completed correctly to avoid issues later on.

Monthly reporting requirements

- Increased pressure on staff at month end may lead initially to resistance to complete the necessary tasks.

- Risk of inaccurate information provided if staff are not trained and motivated to provide quality reports. It is important to explain to staff why this is required, and how it will help the company going forward.

- It is important to establish exactly what the departments need to report on, and where the initial focus will be. It would be a good idea for CCC to focus initially on key areas of weakness, for example cash flow and payments to suppliers, rather than reporting on all variables.

- The current staff has a mixture of accounting experience, with Stefan being a part-qualified accountant. It is important for the directors to ensure that the team are trained and fully understand what information is required. It is likely that CCC will have to invest in training of staff in order to make any changes.

Recruitment of a qualified senior accountant

- There could be resistance to the introduction of a new member of management, especially within the accounting team. This may be perceived by existing staff as a criticism of their current performance, breeding resentment and poor co-operation with the new accountant.

Activity 7: Implementation of a new system

Risks and concerns regarding the new system at CCC	Potential remedial actions
Taking into account the time to train up the staff prior to the new system commencing.	Review the training plan and consider how the staff will be trained. Discuss options with staff. Consider recruitment of temporary staff to cover basic roles whilst the staff are being trained to minimise impact on the day to day running of the business.
Choosing a date when the old system will be switched off and the new system will need to be ready to be working. When are the busiest times of the year? If customers like to have their new carpet in before Christmas it may not be a good idea to put in a new system in November, in the middle of the busy season. Do the staff want to start the new financial year on the new system? This may involve last minute work getting the records ready over the Christmas period.	For CCC, given the lack of staff experience and availability, it would be best to plan the system change well in advance to ensure staff are available, and advance notice can be given to customers (and suppliers).
Is the hardware available (computers, printers, broadband speed to the office) sufficient for the new system? Who will be using the system? Just the accounts office, or will warehouse and the directors also have their own terminals? There are currently only four computers so additional hardware may need to be purchased (or upgrades to latest software). If this is a cloud-based system can the broadband cope with several staff members accessing it at the same time – is the broadband speed sufficient or will there be additional costs here too?	Complete a hardware audit, ensuring all computers are accounted for and that their software is up to date and registered by the business (in particular, the computer used in the warehouse may be an issue here). Consider whether additional costs for new or upgraded hardware are to be included in the tangible costs budget for the project. Review the broadband capacity and consider alternatives if required.

Risks and concerns regarding the new system at CCC	Potential remedial actions
Do the systems need to work 'in parallel' so that any errors can be detected early whilst still maintaining a backup system? Consider how the old system(s) will be archived to prevent unauthorised editing access once the new system has gone live.	In a small organisation like CCC this may be too time consuming and difficult to manage. Propose a hard deadline where the old system is switched off and the new one goes live to minimise confusion with the staff and to reduce inadvertent access to the old system. Ensure the data on the old system is still accessible; however, it cannot be edited.
How will the closing balances from one system be confirmed as correct prior to being set up on the new system and how will the existing data (supplier details, customers etc) be set up on the new system? There may be a resource or skill issue at CCC as the staff work part time and none of them are experienced in changing systems or have sufficient experience to see potential issues.	Cleansing of data prior to migration onto the new system. This will ensure that the new data is accurate – this will take time and staff resources, but once the data is on the new system, then management will have comfort in its accuracy. Management may need to consider using expertise brought in from the local accountancy firm to ensure accuracy and the actions are completed prior to migration.

Note. Ensure that the answers are tailored to the needs of CCC using the scenario and other information eg not just a list of what could go wrong in all scenarios.

Test your learning: answers

Chapter 1 Introduction to the organisation

1

	✓
Fraud Act 2006	
Companies Act 2006	
Bribery Act 2010	
Data Protection Regulations	✓

Data Protection Regulations – state the rules regarding how the organisation processes and stores sensitive information on customers, suppliers and employees.

2 A statement of cash flows shows receipt of a loan as part of **financing activities** and proceeds from the disposal of non-current assets as part of **investing activities**.

3 A bank which has lent money to a company is **an external** stakeholder of the company.

4

	Financial ✓	Ethical ✓	Environmental ✓
Improving recycling rates in the factory by 30% year on year	✓		✓
Changing supplier who can supply the materials 20% cheaper, but with less control over the supply chain	✓	✓	
Installing a carbon capture unit on the main factory costing £2 million	✓		✓
Introducing a more generous pension scheme for employees	✓	✓	

All of the decisions will impact the company on a financial basis, either short term or long term (such as the pension scheme commitments and the carbon capture capital installation). It may be argued that by treating staff more favourably by allowing them access to a better pension scheme, this would be an ethical decision made by the organisation. Equally, changing the supplier to one whose supply chain may be less transparent could help the profitability of an organisation, but may adversely affect its ethical stance (consider the real life examples where high street fashion chains have sourced their clothing from less reputable companies, and faced a harsh public response as a result). Improving recycling rates and reducing carbon emissions will have an environmental impact as well as a financial one.

5   The financial statements of a company must be prepared in accordance with **Companies Act 2006**.

It is the responsibility of the **board of directors** to ensure that these are completed and filed with **the Registrar of Companies** to ensure compliance with that law.

6

	✓
AAT Code of Ethics	✓
Groceries Supply Code of Practice	✓
Auto-enrolment for pensions	
Gender pay gap reporting	

Neither the AAT Code of Ethics nor the Groceries Supply Code of Practice are legal requirements, but they are ethical guidelines. Both gender pay gap reporting and auto-enrolment for pensions are legal requirements.

Chapter 2 The accounting function

1

Scenario	Type
Future demand estimations for the next 12 months	Strategic
Competitor analysis	Strategic
Failure rate report of a machine used in production	Operational
Customer service response times	Operational

2

	✓
A centralised accounting function has better communication with business units than a decentralised one.	
A decentralised accounting function has more economies of scale compared with a centralised one.	
A centralised accounting function has more economies of scope than a decentralised one.	✓
A decentralised accounting function is better placed to produce group accounts than a centralised one.	

3   A company with many layers of management can be described as having a **tall** organisation structure with managers having a **narrow** span of control.

4   **Tactical information** is used to decide how the resources of the business should be deployed, and to monitor how they are being and have been utilised.

5   Production reject rate is an example of **operational** information.

6

	✓
Teamwork	
Managers	
Accounting software	✓
Control environment	

Teamwork and managers will have the most significant impact on the culture of the organisation as they will affect how people collaborate, communicate and work together. The control environment may influence the culture as a stricter or closer monitored set of controls will create a less flexible but more systematic culture. Accounting software is the least likely to affect the culture as this is a tool used by the organisation. The main impact on the culture of an organisation is how strict any system controls may be.

7

	✓
The requirement to prepare statutory accounts at the year end	✓
Preparation of the corporate tax return for the organisation	
Preparation of the payroll for the organisation	
Batch invoice processing for the purchases department in a large organisation	

The requirement to prepare statutory accounts at the year end is set by the Companies Act 2006 and is the responsibility of the directors. This responsibility cannot be outsourced; however, the **preparation** of the accounts may be outsourced. All of the other options either require specialist knowledge which may not be available within an organisation (tax, payroll) or are a routine, low skilled task (batch processing).

Chapter 3 Accounting systems

1   An integrated accounting system is **centralised**. One of its core objectives should be **compliance with laws and regulations**.

2

Activities	Type of security control
Validation of input data	Integrity control
Passwords	System control
Archiving	Physical access control

3

Activities	Type of security control
Batch processing of invoices	Completeness
Only the finance manager can authorise new suppliers on the system	Segregation of duties
Sequential numbering of invoices	Completeness
Alerts to the user when the journal being entered does not balance	Integrity

4

Activities	✓
Cost effectiveness	✓
Ease of use	
Reliable	✓
Providing timely information	✓

Ease of use is not a specific objective of an accounting system although it is fair to say that this would be a desirable feature. The accounting system should meet the requirements of the organisation in providing reliable and timely information in a cost-effective manner.

5   The requirement for an accountant to act diligently is part of the fundamental principle of **professional competence and due care**.

Professional competence and due care: Having the right level of current professional knowledge and skill to give competent professional service and **acting diligently** and in accordance with applicable and professional standards.

Chapter 4 Internal control systems

1

Action	Type of control activity
Person A matches dispatch notes to invoices; Person B creates invoice to customer	Segregation of duties
Control account reconciliation	Arithmetic/bookkeeping check
Petty cash box kept locked	Physical control
Adequate resourcing of accounting function	Organisation
Review of budgetary control report	Management control

2   In SWOT analysis, strengths and weaknesses are **internal to the company** and opportunities and threats are **external to the company**.

3   Management should regularly ensure that staff perform **reconciliations** of the sales ledger to ensure accuracy and completeness of the data.

4   Control objectives in relation to taking orders and extending credit are part of the **sales** sub-system of the accounting system.

5   Completion of GRNs is a control activity related to the control objective of **only accepting goods and services that have been ordered and appropriately authorised**.

6 Allocating one customer's payment to another in order to balance the books and detract from a shortfall is called **teeming and lading**.

Chapter 5 Monitoring controls and detecting fraud

1

	✓
False accounting	
False representation	✓
Misstatement of the financial statements	
Misappropriation of assets	

2 Internal audit activities are a type of **management control** over fraud in the accounting system.

3

	✓
Time	
Responsibility	
Likelihood	✓
Volatility	
Impact	✓

4

	✓
Morale	✓
Social	
Reputation	✓
Environmental	
Financial	✓

5

	✓
During the analysis of the sales system, a fraud matrix graded the potential loss from misappropriation to be rated 5. Management have decided urgent action is required.	✓
A fraud matrix is a subjective analysis of an organisation's controls and will ensure that all recommendations identified are actioned immediately.	
A control within the payroll system has been rated as 2 within the fraud matrix. Management have decided that this risk must be rectified immediately.	

A fraud matrix enables the prioritisation of the key risks, focusing on the most significant first. An organisation will then deal with the highest risks first, which is why a fraud matrix grades the risks rather than dealing with all of the weaknesses at the same time.

A fraud matrix rates the lowest risk as 1 and the highest as 5, therefore anything rated 5 should be prioritised over lower rated risks.

Chapter 6 Making changes to systems

1   Ard Ltd's plan is **a transformational** change.

2

	✓
a tangible cost of the change.	
an intangible benefit of the change.	
a tangible benefit of the change.	
an intangible cost of the change.	✓

3   The fact that Ard Ltd's employees will be disrupted by the planned change, so will not be able to work on an alternative new project, is an **opportunity cost** of the change.

4   This is an example of **a forced** change, and ensuring the system is effective following such a change is likely to take **some time**.

5   Change should be **cost effective** in that the benefits of the change should outweigh its costs.

	Reason
A merger of the treasury and the finance function	Personnel change
Management accounts report that the costs for the warehouse department are consistently running above budget	Financial change
The sales team to be issued with tablet computers to allow them to place orders and check inventory levels, whilst with customers in the showroom	Technological change
The directors are discontinuing one of the less profitable products, resulting in a refocus on the remaining three core products instead	Company strategy change

Scenario

Cookridge & Cookridge Carpets Ltd (CCC) scenario and analysis

Company background and history

Cookridge & Cookridge Carpets Ltd (CCC) is a large carpet and flooring dealership based in Southampton. It is the main dealer in the area for 'Umteeko' specialist vinyl flooring, and has been trading for four years. It was set up by two brothers, Peter and John Cookridge.

Peter is a trained carpet fitter and has worked in the industry for the past 20 years. Before going into business with his brother, he was the senior manager in a national carpet chain. John was recently made redundant from his role as a mining engineer.

The business was established using John's £80,000 redundancy payment and an inheritance the brothers received. Peter managed to raise a loan of £60,000 (using his house as collateral) in 20X2 to refinance the business as the company's bank overdraft was getting large, and expensive to maintain.

The brothers purchased a large plot of land on which they developed a building to use as the carpet and flooring showroom. They started out selling and fitting carpets, and then expanded into specialist flooring. This expansion was organised by Peter, who had developed excellent working relationships with carpet and vinyl manufacturers from his time in the industry.

In February 20X1, CCC was asked by Umteeko to become its main dealership for Southampton. Umteeko is a quality product commanding a premium price and requires fitters to have specialist training to fit it.

CCC's mission statement

Our mission is to provide an excellent level of service to all of our customers – and we endeavour to offer our customers a quality product at a competitive price.

We aim to act ethically towards our suppliers, customers and staff, ensuring the best in service and supporting diverse needs and requirements.

The environment is important to us and we aim to recycle wherever possible; we promise to remove all of the packaging from customers' premises and dispose of this in an environmentally friendly way.

Developments in the market

The popularity of Umteeko has grown, and therefore the supplier insists on reviewing its dealers on a regular basis. All fitters must be fully trained, and qualified fitters are required to attend a refresher course every two years. Umteeko requires that only its specialist adhesives are used in the fitting process to ensure its product guarantees are valid.

Carpets are declining in popularity in the UK market with the rise of allergies, and the difficulties of keeping carpets clean in a busy family home. Wood and laminate flooring, as well as specialist vinyl floors like Umteeko and its main competitor, Kleandarn, are increasing their market share.

The increase in large warehouse-style retailers has reduced smaller retailers' margins on many of the popular brands of carpet and vinyl. CCC is finding it hard to match the prices of the larger retailers on some of the products it is selling.

CCC's strategic planning and control

Strategy mapping

Strategy maps are tools used by organisations to consider how value is created. They evaluate connections between strategic objectives in the form of causes and effects.

Staff

CCC's key personnel are as follows:

Director	John Cookridge
Director	Peter Cookridge
Wages Clerk	Sonja Douglas (part-time)
Accounts Clerk	Margaret Peterson
Accounts Receivable Clerk	Stefan Kalinowski (part time)
Showroom and Marketing Manager	Jim Andrews
Warehouse and Operations Manager	Joe Bloggins (joined October 20X2)
Sales staff	Isaac Jackson Ron Sellers Kim Lee
Delivery drivers	Sasha Bilton Lynn Smith
Carpet fitters	Jake Brew Pritpal Iqbal John Smedley David Lee Paul Collins (also can fit vinyl and wood floors)
Vinyl fitters	Sally Burroughs (Umteeko trained) Alan Rogers (Umteeko trained) Jack Brundell

Peter's main hobby is building and racing motorbikes. He is a popular and well-known figure on the local motor racing scene.

John is married to Paula, who acted as company secretary for the first two years of the company's existence. She then left CCC to train as a solicitor.

The financial statements have been prepared by a local accountancy firm, Bright & Co; however, the directors are planning on bringing the preparation of these within CCC's accounting department. The company does not require an audit.

Extracts from the financial statements of CCC as at 31 December 20X2

Statement of profit or loss for CCC for the year ended 31 December 20X2

	20X2 £000	20X1 £000
Revenue	1,106	930
Cost of sales	(703)	(633)
Gross profit	403	297
Salaries	(312)	(257)
Rent and rates	(30)	(30)
Other costs	(54)	(28)
Profit/loss from operations	**7**	**(18)**
Finance costs	(5)	(6)
Profit/loss before tax	**2**	**(24)**
Tax	–	–
Profit/loss for the period	**2**	**(24)**

Statement of financial position for CCC as at 31 December 20X2

	20X2 £000	20X1 £000
ASSETS		
Non-current assets	78	83
Current assets		
Inventory	85	61
Trade receivables	134	83
Bank and cash on hand	2	4
Total assets	**299**	**231**

	20X2 £000	20X1 £000
EQUITY AND LIABILITIES		
Share capital	1	1
Retained earnings	65	63
Total equity	66	64
Non-current liabilities		
Loan	60	–
Current liabilities		
Trade payables	131	86
Bank overdraft	37	78
Accruals and other payables	5	3
Total liabilities	**299**	**231**

Extracts from the management accounts for year ending 31 December 20X2

	20X2		20X1	
	Carpets £000	Vinyl £000	Carpets £000	Vinyl £000
Revenue	379	727	425	505
Cost of sales (including materials and staff)	(287)	(416)	(282)	(351)
Gross margin	**92**	**311**	**143**	**154**

	£000	£000	£000	£000
Rent and rates	30		30	
Salaries: administration and management	87		87	
Salaries: sales	105		60	
Salaries: directors	120		110	
Motor expenses	19		10	
Irrecoverable debts	22		8	
Other costs	18		16	
Total costs		**401**		**321**
Net profit/(loss)		**2**		**(24)**

Other operational information

The carpet showroom's opening hours are as follows:

- Open six days a week
- Operates from 9:00am until 9:00pm, Monday to Saturday

The accounting function works from 9:00am until 5:30pm, Monday to Friday.

The accounting function office is located on the first floor of the showroom. Access to the office is by a set of stairs at the rear of the building. Toilet facilities for staff and customers are also on the first floor, so the stairs are used by members of the public.

Once on this floor, access to the accounting function office is easy because the keypad lock is never used – the accounts staff prefer to keep the door propped open. The accounting function office is open plan, with no private working areas.

Both the brothers are key holders for the business. They hold the only full sets of keys, as one of them is always on the premises at close of business to ensure the property is secure. There is an alarm code they set every evening when they lock up.

Finance team

The accounting staff use three computers (using a business version of Microsoft) which were purchased when the company was set up. In addition, a further two computers were purchased last year which are used by the warehouse team. The warehouse manager used the installation key from his home software to install an older version of Microsoft on the new computers to save the company some money.

Excel spreadsheets are used for the bookkeeping and payroll calculations (HMRC tax tables are used by Sonja to ensure the correct tax is calculated). Stefan uses a template in Word to produce and print out sales invoices.

The sales team place orders manually which go to Stefan who raises invoices. Customers are booked in for fitting (if required) or delivery.

Stefan backs up his sales data onto a small, separate hard drive. He has set up similar ones for payroll and purchases but is unsure whether Margaret and Sonja regularly use them. The aged receivables report is compiled by Stefan who enters the invoices onto an Excel spreadsheet. Any unpaid invoices which are over 35 days late are sent to a debt collection agency.

The finance team prepare quarterly management accounts, and these are given to management by the 20th of the month following the quarter end. The management accounts include a basic summary of the revenue and costs for the period, a budget control report and any other information requested by the management team; sometimes it is the aged receivables ledger and sometimes it is a review of the payroll costs.

Fitting team

The delivery dates are set up by the sales team and discussed with the operations manager.

The fitters are then given a set amount of time to fit the flooring based on the product they are fitting; however, not all of the fitters work to the same standard and some are quicker than others. Some of the Umteeko fitters complain that there is not enough time to follow the full procedures required of the product.

Glossary of terms

It is useful to be familiar with interchangeable terminology including IFRS and UK GAAP (generally accepted accounting principles).

Below is a short list of the most important terms you are likely to use or come across, together with their international and UK equivalents.

UK term	International term
Profit and loss account	**Statement of profit or loss (or statement of profit or loss and other comprehensive income)**
Turnover or sales	Revenue or sales revenue
Operating profit	Profit from operations
Reducing balance depreciation	Diminishing balance depreciation
Depreciation/depreciation expense(s)	Depreciation charge(s)
Balance sheet	**Statement of financial position**
Fixed assets	Non-current assets
Net book value	Carrying amount
Tangible assets	Property, plant and equipment
Stocks	Inventories
Trade debtors or debtors	Trade receivables
Prepayments	Other receivables
Debtors and prepayments	Trade and other receivables
Cash at bank and in hand	Cash and cash equivalents
Long-term liabilities	Non-current liabilities
Trade creditors or creditors	Trade payables
Accruals	Other payables
Creditors and accruals	Trade and other payables
Capital and reserves	Equity (limited companies)
Profit and loss balance	Retained earnings
Cash flow statement	**Statement of cash flows**

Accountants often have a tendency to use several phrases to describe the same thing! Some of these are listed below:

Different terms for the same thing
Nominal ledger, main ledger or general ledger
Subsidiary ledgers, memorandum ledgers
Subsidiary (sales) ledger, sales ledger
Subsidiary (purchases) ledger, purchases ledger

Bibliography

AAT (2017) *Code of Professional Ethics.* [Online]. Available from: www.aat.org.uk [Accessed 17 June 2021].

Financial Conduct Authority (2019) *FCA fines Standard Chartered Bank £102.2 million for poor AML controls.* [Online]. Available from: www.fca.org.uk/news/search-results?np_category=press%20releases&start=1 [Accessed 17 June 2021].

Reuters (2017) *Tesco to pay £214m to settle false accounting charges* [Online]. Available from: http://uk.reuters.com [Accessed 17 June 2021]

Jaguar Land Rover (2016) *Responsibility.* [Online]. Available from: www.jaguar.co.uk/about-jaguar/responsibility [Accessed 17 June 2021].

Serious Fraud Office (2017) *SFO completes £497.25m Deferred Prosecution Agreement with Rolls-Royce PLC.* [Online]. Available from: www.sfo.gov.uk/cases/rolls-royce-plc [Accessed 17 June 2021].

Farmers Weekly (2019) Retailer Watch: *Which supermarket treats suppliers the best?* [Online] Available from: https://www.fwi.co.uk/business/retailer-watch-supermarket-treats-suppliers-best [Accessed 17 June 2021]

John Lewis Partnership PLC, *Annual Report and Accounts 2018* (2018) [Online] Available from: https://www.johnlewispartnership.co.uk/financials/financial-results.html [Accessed 17 June 2021]

AAT (2016), *Accounting for good* (2016) [Online] Available from: https://www.aat.org.uk/prod/s3fs-public/assets/Accounting-for-good-report-FINAL.pdf [Accessed 17 June 2021]

EY (2014), *Integrated reporting: Elevating value* [Online] Available from: https://www.ey.com/en_vn/ey-publications [Accessed 17 June 2021]

Index

A

AAT
  Code of Professional Ethics, 55
Accounting controls, 68
Accounting function, 28
  Boots, 30
  Centralisation, 34
  Culture, 33
  Ethical considerations, 33
  Levels of management, 30
  Marks and Spencer, 30
  NHS, 32
  Objectives, 28
  Organisation, 28
  Outsourcing, 36
  Policies, 33
  Structure, 28
  Tall or flat organisation, 30
  Working practices, 34
Accounting system controls, 50
  Ethical risks, 57
  Security, 52
Accounting system controls
  Control environment, 66
  Limitations, 83
  Payroll system controls, 78–81
  Purchase system controls, 75–78
  Sales system controls, 70–75
  Systemic weaknesses, 66
Accounting system controls
  Monitoring controls, 92, 99, 101
Accounting systems, 48
  Objectives, 48
Accounting transactions, 28
Accounting transactions
  Raw data, 48
Application controls, 52
Authorisation controls, 68
Authorisation of transactions, 68, **71**

B

Boots. *See* Accounting function
Budgetary control report, 103, 105
Budgetary slack, 34

C

Centralised accounting function, 34
Companies Act 2006, 8

Companies and Limited Liability Partnerships
  (Energy and Carbon Report) Regulations
  2018, 18
Confidentiality, **55**
Control activities, 66, **67**
Control environment, 66
Control objectives, 70
Controls during transition. *See* Implementation
  of new system
Corporate Social Reporting (CSR), 14
  Jaguar Land Rover, 14
Corporate social responsibility statements, 14
Cost effectiveness, **48**, 118
Cost-benefit analysis, **122**
  Intangible, 126
  Opportunity costs, 126
  Relevant costs, 126
  Tangible costs and benefits, 122
Culture, **32**, 33
  Ethical values, 33
  Influences on the system, 55
  policies, 33

D

Decentralised accounting functions. *See*
  Centralised accounting function
Decision making, 38, 75
Documenting the system, 50
  Flowcharts, 50–51
  User manual, 51

E

Ethical budgeting, 34
Ethical reporting, 15
  Economic aspects, 33
  Environmental aspects, 33
  Social aspects, 33
  Equality and Diversity, 18
  Social responsibility. *See* Corporate Social
    Reporting (CSR)
Ethical treatment of suppliers, 15
Ethical values, 56, 60
Ethics, **56**, 57, 58
  Conflict, 58
External reporting requirements, 9
  Regulation changes, 120

F

Financial accounting, 30, 42
Financial Conduct Authority (FCA), 95

Flowchart. *See* Documenting the system
Fraud, 92, **93**
  Controls, 96
  Detection, 101
  Impact, 95
  Misappropriation of assets, 93
  Misstatement of the financial statements, 93, 95
  Payroll system, 99
  Purchases system, 98
  Rolls-Royce PLC, 95
  Sales system, 96–97
  Standard Chartered, 95
  Tesco, 95
Fraud
  Detection, 66
  Misappropriation of assets, 70
Fraud Act 2006, 93
Fraud matrix, 108
Fundamental principles, 55
Fundamental principles of professional ethics, 55

G

Goal congruence, 34
Groceries Supply Code of Practice, 15, 23

I

Implementation of new system, 134
  Controls during transition, 132
Incremental change, 121
Industry regulations, 18
Industry regulations
  Changes impacting operation, 120
Intangible benefits, 127
Intangible costs, 126
Integrated accounting systems, 54
Integrated reporting, 16
Integrity, **55**
Integrity controls, 52
Integrity of data, **52**
Internal control system, 66
Internal controls, 50, 66
  Accounting controls, 68
  Authorisation, 68
  Control environment. See Accounting system controls
  Organisation, 56, 68
  Personnel controls, 68
  Physical controls, 68
  Segregation of duties, 67, 70
  SPAMSOAP, 67

Internal reporting requirements, 13
  Management accounting, 12, 13

J

John Lewis Partnership. *See* Real Life Example

L

Legislative regulations, 18, 128
  Accounting standards, 120
  Bribery Act 2010, 18
  Data Protection Regulations, 18
  Fraud Act 2006, 18
  IFRS 15 *Revenue*, 120
  Late payment law, 18
  Money Laundering Regulations 2007, 120
  Public Interest Disclosure Act 1998, 18
  'Real Time Information' (RTI), 120
  The Proceeds of Crime Act 2002, 18
  Weakness and recommendations, 121
Level of risk. *See* Fraud matrix
Limitations of internal control systems, 83

M

Management accounting, 30
Management accounts
  Budgetary control reports, 103
  Ratio analysis, 105
  Review process, 101
Management information, 37
Management information systems (MIS), 37
  Industry sectors, 38
  Operational information, 38
  Strategic information, 38
  Tactical information, 38
Marks & Spencer. *See* Accounting function
Mission statement, 14, 56
Money Laundering Regulations, 12
  Money Laundering, Terrorist Financing and Transfer of Funds, 18
Monitoring controls, 92, 99, 101, 128

N

Need for change
  Cost-benefit analysis, 122–33
  Justification, 128
  Regulations, 120
  Resistance, 131
NHS. *See* Accounting function
Non-financial measures. *See* Scorecards
Non-Financial Reporting Directive 2014, 18

Not for profit organisations, 29

O

Objectivity, **55**
Operational information, **38**
Opportunity cost, 126
Outsourcing, 36

P

Payroll system controls, 78–81
    Fraud, 99
Performance measurement, 38, 75
Physical controls, **52**, 68
Planning. *See* Management information
Preventing errors, 53
Processing controls, 53
Professional behaviour, **55**
Professional competence and due care, 55
Professional competence and due care, **55**
Purchase system controls, 75–78
    Fraud, 98

R

Ratio analysis, 68, 105
Raw data, 127, *See* Accounting transactions
Real Life Example
    Jaguar Land Rover, 14
    John Lewis Partnership, 16
    NHS, 32
    Rolls-Royce PLC, 95
    Standard Chartered, 95
    Tesco, 95
Reconciliations, **68**
Registrar of Companies. *Companies Act 2006*
Relevant costs. See Cost-benefit analysis
Reliability, **49**
Reviews, **68**
Risk, **66**
Risk assessment, 66, 85, 99
    Grading, 109
Risk assessment process, **81**, 100
Risk of fraud, 99
Rolls-Royce PLC. *See* Fraud
RTI, 12

S

Sales system controls, 70–75
    Fraud, 96

Scorecard, **106**, 107
Sector analysis, 39
Segregation of duties, 52, 67, 70, 75, 78, 98
Serious Fraud Office (SFO). *See* Fraud
Size of the organisation, 29–30
Stakeholder, **4**, 105
    Ethical and sustainable practices, 13
    Ethical practice, 56
    Expectations, 5
    External stakeholders, 8
    Internal stakeholders, 7
    Other reporting requirements, 13
Standard Chartered. *See* Fraud
Statement of cash flows, 9, 11
Statement of financial position, 9
Statement of profit or loss, 9
Statutory financial statements
    Key purposes, 9–10
Stewardship. *See* Statutory financial statements
Strategic information, **38**
Structure, **28**
Sustainability reporting. *See* Ethical reporting
SWOT analysis, 81
System flowchart, 50

T

Tactical information, **38**
Tall and flat organisation structures. *See* Accounting Function
Tangible benefits, 127
Tangible cost & benefit, 122
Tax incentives, 13
Taxation regulations, 18
Teeming and lading, 71
Tesco. *See* Fraud
Timeliness, **49**
Transaction processing, 30
Transformational change, 121
Treasury management, 30

U

US Department of Justice, 95
User manuals. *See* Documenting the system

V

VAT, 12

Notes

Notes